OUTSIDE

THE

LAW

EDITED BY

SUSAN RICHARDS SHREVE

AND PORTER SHREVE

OUTSIDE

THE

LAW

NARRATIVES ON

JUSTICE IN AMERICA

BEACON PRESS

BOSTON

BEACON PRESS
25 Beacon Street
Boston, Massachusetts 02108-2892

BEACON PRESS BOOKS
are published under the auspices
of the Unitarian Universalist Association of Congregations.

02 01 00 99 98 97   8 7 6 5 4 3 2 1

Text design by Elizabeth Elsas

Library of Congress Cataloging-in-Publication Data

Outside the law: narratives on justice in America/edited by Susan
    Richards Shreve and Porter Shreve.
        p. cm.
    ISBN 0-8070-4406-7 (cloth)
    1. Justice, Administration of—United States. 2. Law—United
States. I. Shreve, Susan Richards. II. Shreve, Porter.
KF384.093 1997
349. 73—DC21   96–47163

CONTENTS

v

CONTENTS

PREFACE

"Outside the law" brings to mind a picture of justice as revenge—the mysterious stranger who appears on the scene, from the hills or out of the shadows, coming to right the balance when the system has failed: the masked man, the vigilante, now playing at a theater near you.

It did not seem an ideal choice, therefore, for the title of this book. We wanted something classic, something with weight; even the subtitle standing alone felt more appropriate, simply *Narratives on Justice in America*. That's what this is, after all, some of our best contemporary writers taking on one of the grand ideas. Thoughtful essays on the subject of justice, essays that add new voice to an old conversation.

This wasn't to be a book about revenge. If anything, we expected the opposite. Narrative writing is by nature empathetic. It invites us in to experience other lives, dissolving, at least until the end of the story, the prejudicial layers of race, class, culture, and region. In this way, stories work like no other form, capturing the emotions, allowing us to imagine ourselves in different circumstances, as different people, broadening our understanding and compassion. We chose storytellers with this idea in mind—to give justice a face, to make a distant concept personal.

As the essays arrived, something surprising happened. "Outside the law" kept announcing itself, not as the stranger from the hills, not as revenge but as a way of understanding justice, a connection point for a wide range of perspectives. If there was one thing everyone seemed to be saying, it was this: Justice *is* outside the law.

"Law is a frail human concept, an agreement, slowly or carelessly or fearfully arrived at, to protect human expectations," writes Richard Bausch in his essay, "A Confession."

Mutable, absurdly arbitrary and uneven, but nevertheless tangible across the grid of time.

Justice is something else. It's all over the place, individualized, as Madison Smartt Bell explains. Every one of us believes that we know right from wrong, that within us dwells a kind of "true morality." And therein lies the problem: "One's inner sense of justice appears to be so axiomatic that only extraordinary circumstances can move one to question whether it is absolutely true or whether it is shared by any or many others."

Beyond a clear consensus among the writers that justice by definition is outside the law was the surprising frequency in the essays of the word "outside" itself: "outside" as opposed to "inside," "them" as opposed to "us," words that underscored the difference between what is hoped for—justice—and what is available—the law.

For Julia Alvarez, fleeing a dictatorship at the age of ten, the law was one man, General Trujillo, and justice a dangerous notion that she could only consider from the outside, as an immigrant in America.

In Charles Johnson's short story about affirmative action, the head of a Seattle company is faced with an "executive decision"— whether to hire a white woman from a similar social station or a black man who is equally qualified but guarded and unfamiliar, outside of the company executive's experience.

Outside and inside and who occupies which place is the subject of Sarah Pettit's essay, "Justify Our Love," which suggests that, as a group, gays in America are neither outside nor inside the system. "Trapped somewhere in the cogs of justice," she writes, "we are plates that don't fit."

Prison, the ultimate "inside" for those the justice system wishes to keep out, is the emotional center of a number of the essays.

In John Edgar Wideman's "Justice: A Perspective," the incarceration of the author's juvenile son for murder and his subsequent sentencing to life without parole reveals "how law dismembers, tears apart living tissue."

For Beverly Lowry, a long period of mourning her son's death in a hit-and-run "occurrence" that she still refuses to call an "accident" leads to an unlikely friendship with a young woman on death row and a new understanding of hope.

"It is no longer fashionable to imprison in full view, we now banish to the far-flung corners of the earth," writes Daniel J. Wideman in "Free Papers." "The way a society distances itself from physical structures . . . mirrors the way narratives of history and justice bury, evade, and marginalize."

Such was the case for Garrett Hongo, whose father fought in Europe during World War II while his grandfather was sent to an internment camp. In his essay, "HR 442: Redress," Hongo writes of justice delayed to Japanese Americans "banished" by the U.S. government because of their race.

A different kind of "evasion" and "marginalization" is explored in Alex Kotlowitz's "Where Was the Village?" Two boys, aged ten and eleven, are sent to prison for dropping their five-year-old neighbor to his death from a fourteenth-floor window. Kotlowitz goes to the Ida B. Wells public housing complex on Chicago's South Side, finding truth in the old aphorism, "It takes a village to raise a child."

While it is possible to connect all of the essays to a single thesis, to do so would diminish the book. The writers take on a wide range of ideas, and no single notion, even one as adaptable as "justice is outside the law," could begin to tie the collection neatly together. What the essays do more than anything is to begin the debate, ask provocative questions, challenge readers to come up with their own narratives on justice.

"Where did we ever get the idea that life is ultimately fair?" asks Michael Dorris in the first lines of "The Myth of Justice." "Who promised that there was a balance to things, a yin and yang that perfectly cancels each other out, a divine score sheet that makes sure that all the totals eventually ring even? Who exactly reaps what they sow?"

Dorris's tone is one that we recognize, familiar and conversational. It engages us, drawing us in, taking us on—What do you think of this?, it seems to say. Justice is a myth. Prove otherwise.

So too with Ntozake Shange: "I want to make some noise and bash some heads. Run the Boers into the sea. Take all the Ashante art out the basement of the British Museum, out the basement of the Met for that matter. When I talk about what I imagine to be just, I sound like a crazy wild niggah roaming the streets and dangerous to American 'civilization.'"

And when the tone isn't provocative, the implications are. Blanche McCrary Boyd in "Who Killed Susan Smith?" mixes reportage with morality play and finds sympathy for the mother who drowned her two young sons, showing how the town of Union, South Carolina, may have been complicitous in her guilt.

For Clarence Page, the controversy is in the subject matter. He writes about jury nullification, "a jury's power to neutralize laws it believes to be unjust, even when it frees the guilty." Page begins with the O. J. Simpson case, exploring whether the jury ignored evidence in reaching its verdict.

In "The Silent Juror," Susan Richards Shreve offers a primary text on how juries make decisions, giving a fictionalized account of a trial she once participated in. We go inside the deliberation room, where a group of jurors are torn between sympathy for a young defendant and a duty to uphold the law.

Like jurors, the contributors to *Outside the Law*, with few exceptions, have no ties to the justice system. They are writers, observers, themselves outside the law. But unlike jurors, unlike judges and lawyers, police and detectives, prison officials and parole board members, unlike national, state and local politicians and all others serving or legislating the law, writers work in a purely moral realm; to tell stories of justice or injustice, unfettered by duty, advocacy, rule or procedure, is their particular privilege.

According to John Casey, it is their obligation. Casey once had ties to the justice system, but after graduating from Harvard Law School, he became a writer. In "Justice as a Nourisher of Narrative," he weaves examples in literature, from the Old Testament, Shakespeare, Henry James, and James Joyce, to demonstrate how the best fiction is informed by a thorough understanding of justice.

Gerald M. Stern is the only practicing legal professional among the contributors. An attorney who began his career trying voter discrimination cases in the civil rights South, his essay is a remembrance of those years, in particular his battles with a determined racist judge, William Harold Cox, of Mississippi Federal District Court.

We asked the legal scholar Martha Minow of Harvard Law School to write the introduction to *Outside the Law*. Herself an insider, Professor Minow, as much as anyone in her field, knows the value of the outsider's perspective.

"Looking at instances plucks, and tunes, a sense of injustice," she writes. "Narratives with a human voice, moving through time and specific places, can convey complex layers of feelings and strands of causes. . . . Stories of injustice do not simply trigger emotions; they inform and educate passion and compassion."

These narratives on justice are a beginning. See how they move you, as you recall your own.

PORTER SHREVE

MARTHA MINOW

INTRODUCTION: SEEKING JUSTICE

The ruminative essays in this book restore vitality to the phrase "beautifully written"; they evoke insights, shivers, rage, tears. Reading the essays attune both a sense of justice and a commitment to pursue it, in ways that do so better than some other endeavors, such as studying law or philosophy. This conclusion follows six steps of argument.

1. DON'T LEAVE JUSTICE TO LAWYERS

After students in my law school courses have finished about a month of law school, I ask them why none of them ever mentions the "j" word. When I relieve their perplexity by divulging it means justice, they laugh nervously, but still don't mention it. Somehow, law school quickly gives the message that law is not about justice. Justice is for the sentimental, the immature, or, in any case, not for lawyers.

The most explicit hoary statements of this view came from Oliver Wendell Holmes Jr., a longtime state judge and U.S. Supreme Court justice as well as theorist of law. In one published letter, he recounted, "I have said to my brethren many times that I hate justice, which means that I know if a man begins to talk about that, for one reason or another he is shirking thinking in legal terms."[1] Similarly,

---

1. Letter to Dr. John C. Wu, July 1, 1929, quoted in Michael Hertz, "Do Justice!: Variations of a Thrice-Told Tale," *Virginia Law Review* 82 (1996): 111, 114 & n. 9.

Judge Learned Hand (what was his mother thinking when she named him?) first told the story about the time he accompanied Justice Holmes on his way to the courthouse and said in farewell, "Do justice!" only to be scolded by Holmes who replied, "That is not my job. My job is to apply the law."[2]

Cited most commonly for the notion that judging is about enforcing existing rules, Holmes's view could mean that law has little to do with justice. But it also could embrace a particular view of justice or, at least, justice under law: Justice is promoted by the consistent application of known rules, which in turn can guide conduct and make punishment predictable.

Many within the legal world find either version of Holmes's view inadequate, or simply wrong. For them, law must be about justice to be legitimate. Or law must be about justice because the parties, the issues, the structure of reasoned debate and commitment to fairness bring issues of justice constantly to the fore. Thus, Abram Chayes explicitly repudiates Justice Holmes's view and concludes, "We know that law is inevitably concerned with justice."[3] Judge John Noonan argues that lawyers and judges should not try to hide behind the role of the professional to avoid responsibility for justice.[4]

The debate becomes even more complex when lawyering, as well as judging, is addressed. If the system calls for adversary advocacy, lawyers may justify zealous work on behalf of venal, guilty clients. If those clients prevail, justice in the particular case may be defeated, but the system itself protected. Not many lawyers take the legal system on as itself a threat to justice, although scholars discuss the issue.[5]

2. Ibid., at 111. Hertz has carefully tracked down multiple versions of this story and analyzed the ways in which the version depart from the original versions. In so doing, Hertz has done his own sort of justice, in the sense of pursuing truth *and* attending to the purposes and meanings of human beings in varied contexts.

3. Abram Chayes, "How Does the Court Establish Justice?" *Harvard Law Review* 101 (1988): 1026, 1041.

4. John Noonan, *Persons and Masks of the Law:* Cardoza, Holmes, Jefferson, Wythe as Makers of the Masks (New York: Farrar Straus Giroux, 1976).

5. See David Luban, *Lawyers and Justice: An Ethical Study* (Princeton, N. J.: Princeton University Press 1988); William Simon, "Ethical Discretion in Lawyering," *Harvard Law Review* 101 (1988): 1083; David Wilkins, "Legal Realism for Lawyers," *Harvard Law Review* 104 (1990): 468.

The very existence of debate among legal types about the place of justice in the enterprise of law should serve as a sobering reminder that justice cannot be left in the hands of lawyers or judges. It is too big, too important, too close to private meanings and public purposes, and too much missing to be delegated to any subgroup. The day-to-day conduct of law affords an even more wrenching reminder.

2. DON'T LEAVE JUSTICE TO PHILOSOPHERS

Thus far, I have taken for granted the meaning of justice. But what is justice? If lawyers debate whether it falls within their province, philosophers spend time addressing the meaning of justice, at least as a conceptual matter. They offer distinctions and definitions. Western philosophers contrast corrective, retributive, and distributive justice.[6] Corrective justice seeks to remedy or restore a loss. Retributive justice seeks to punish, avenge, and deter crime or other violations of norms. Distributive justice addresses allocations of resources and opportunities across society.

For each of the types of justice, philosophers debate whether social utility—maximizing the benefits for the greatest number of people—figures largely, exclusively, or not at all in the quest for justice. Thus, utility-maximizers argue that the adoption or enforcement of any rule should be assessed in terms of the costs it imposes, compared with the benefits it actually achieves. Their critics maintain that this method risks reducing all of human values to quantifiable factors and subordinating the integrity and dignity of particular individuals to the needs or desires of majorities.

Philosophers who agree on basic terms nonetheless find much room for disagreement about goals and values. Rivaling the utility goal are notions of virtue, individual autonomy and dignity, and other theories of the good that go beyond social utility. Philosophers also dispute whether justice represents a universal ideal or instead a notion subject to vast cultural variety and specificity. The discussions, useful to a point, nonetheless tend to be quite abstract,

---

6. See, e.g., Robert C. Solomon and Mark C. Murphy, eds., *What is Justice? Classic and Contemporary Readings* (New York: Oxford University Press, 1990).

with little evocation of particular, breathing, bleeding people. Indeed, the philosophic discussions tend to operate on the level of societal design, rather than individual instances, and thus remain remote from the decisions most people make.

3. TRY INJUSTICE

Perhaps it is easier to know what injustice is. Instances of unfairness, mistreatment, and oppression may seem clear precisely because they are instances: specific occasions, involving particular people, actions, and events. Consider these:

> A corporation blows up a plant it has decided not to operate even though the workers proposed to buy it in order to continue its work and their jobs.[7]

> A group of ranchers recruit cheap labor from across the national border and, when the picking season is over, the same ranchers participate in sending the workers back for lacking proper immigration papers.[8]

> Individual employees and the companies that employ them deny dumping any toxic substances in a community that witnesses a sharp increase in cancer rates and in the birth of children with disabilities; an investigative reporter exposes the years of dumping practices after victims and their families settle the lawsuit for very little.[9]

> Four men serve more than sixty years among them in prison for a crime they did not commit, *and* three journalism students exonerate them after uncovering a file withheld from the defense by the prosecution.[10]

7. See Joseph William Singer, "The Reliance Interest in Property," *Stanford Law Review* 40 (1988): 611 (discussing United States Steel Company's demolition of two steel plants in Youngstown, Ohio).

8. See Gerald Lopez, "In Search of a Justice Immigration Law and Policy," *UCLA Law Review* 28 (1981): 615.

9. See Jonathan Harr, *A Civil Action* (New York: Random House, 1995).

10. John Carpenter, "Hard Work Helps Bring Justice to 4 Innocent Men," *Chicago Sun-Times,* 23 June 1996, p. 26.

A sense of injustice rises up when I hear about these instances. I feel outrage, specific to each circumstance, though the outrage offers clues to more general ideas. I'll try to state some of the general ideas:

> It is wrong to punish innocent people; it is even worse when evidence that could save them is withheld or not difficult to find, but no one made the right effort at the right time. It is unfair that these mistakes more likely occur when the defendants are poor and have dark skin. It is unacceptable to have a criminal justice system and a nation thoroughly marked by racial suspicion.

> It is wrong for people to lie about or hide their misconduct that hurts others. Using people when it is convenient and discarding them when it is not violates decency and human dignity; setting people up for punishment after they have served your purposes is unconscionable. Destroying material that could help others be self-sufficient injects cruelty into unfairness.

Stated in such general terms, the principles almost seem vapid, and surely are incomplete. Stating them does not particularly motivate a sense of outrage. There is something about seeing and hearing violations of basic ideals enacted in life, with actual bodily and spiritual consequences, that alerts and refines the sense of injustice. Trials of injustice work best for me not merely as tests of general propositions but as tests for my own capacity to sense what is wrong and to push what must be changed.

Looking at instances plucks, and tunes, a sense of injustice. Narratives with a human voice, moving through time and specific places, can convey complex layers of feelings and strands of causes. They also show where the rubber hits the road. What does a perfect theory of justice matter if it operates miles above human experience? Stories of injustice do not simply trigger emotions; they inform and educate passion and compassion.

Stories of injustice help in another way. It seems easier to see departures from a seldom or never achieved goal than to define the goal itself. Aviam Soifer recently wrote, "Seeking justice is like going east. You can go east and go east as much as you would like—but you never get east."[11]

The search for justice takes time. It takes many participants in many particular places. Lawyers and judges, yes, but also citizen jurors, journalists, voters, teachers, employers, parents, victims who become protesters, noncitizens who claim the status of person.[12] Injustice occurs in daily exchanges, not just cataclysmic events. So must justice be sought when strangers bump bodies on the subway, interview one another for jobs, grade one another, form impressions upon first glance.

The Talmud directs that a judge should feel as though a sword were suspended above his head throughout the time he sits in judgment.[13] The judge and the judged are simultaneously implicated in justice. Stories about failed justice and injustice alert us all and make us better equipped for the search.

4. COMPARE MISFORTUNE AND JUSTICE

I don't know who said it, but it stuck with me. "A civilization progresses when what was viewed as a misfortune becomes viewed as an injustice." It once seemed natural or inevitable that women were viewed as unfit voters, marines, or public officeholders; it once seemed a sad fact of fate that women could not have jobs as violinists or electricians. Before anything else changed, these perceptions changed. People used politics, fiction, public protest, and law to expose these exclusions as injustices. Then, in the name of justice, people struggled for, and in many cases won, change.

If it once seemed the deal of the cards, at least to those who called the shots, that people with dark skin and ancestors from Africa lacked moral capacities, intelligence, rights to enter into

11.   Aviam Soifer, "Who Took the Awe Out of Law?" Graven Images 3 (November 1996):—.
      In the same passage, Soifer notes Holmes's own inconsistencies on the subject.
12.   Under the U.S. Constitution, the basic guarantees of equal protection and due process are assured to persons, not just to citizens. See Fourteenth Amendment, U.S. Constitution.
13.   Quoted in *The Pentateuch and Haftorahs,* 2d ed., ed. J. H. Hertz. (London: Soncino Press, 1960), 500.

contracts, to vote, to serve as mayors, corporate presidents, or a U.S. president, then the dealer had to be exposed as crooked. Injustice, not misfortune, was its name. Injustice may even seem too mild for what might be better known as oppression. What injustice and oppression share is condemnation for violations of human dignity committed by other human beings, violations that are in no way required or inevitable.

Thus, a crucial, though not sufficient, element of justice reimagines misfortunes as injustices. It transforms the "natural" hand of fate into features of a human world that could and should be changed. This is the strategy pursued by those who seek justice in the name of people with disabilities, people who favor sexual relationships with someone who shares their sex, people who want to protect the environment against the ravages of industry and economic development, and people who seek protections for animals. Both sides in the debate over the "right to choose" an abortion and the "right to life" for fetuses claim injustice.

Denaturalize injustice. Harms are not just fate, are not just inevitable. Neither are harms injustice without some element of human choice. Injustice involves people's treatment of others. Tornadoes or earthquakes or other acts of God do not qualify (though even these would amount to injustice if people could have acted differently, could have not built the houses on the fault line, could have not failed to pitch in to share the costs of devastation). Injustice points to something that could have been different, if only people had acted differently. Injustice shows something amenable to protest, struggle, and change.

5. REMEMBER, TOO MUCH JUSTICE IS ALSO INJUSTICE

This may be a play on words, but it's an important point illuminated by Greek tragedies, as well as by the recent experiences of Eastern European nations struggling after toppling Communist regimes.[14] In the rage against oppressive pasts, people running new

14. Tina Rosenberg, *The Haunted Land: Facing Europe's Ghosts after Communism* (New York: Vintage Books, 1995).

regimes tried to purge from government anyone tainted by the old regimes. In the process of trying to clean house, they made new messes. People were purged even if their names appeared in files invented by lazy spies, even if they spent their entire lives in resistance. People were purged to satisfy a quenchless thirst for vengeance—and to open up jobs for others, no more deserving.

The forms used to seek justice thus can be infected by the very cruelties and frailities that produce injustice. Estranged spouses call state child protection agencies to trigger child abuse investigations against one another, deploying the invasive and frightening power of the government in their private combat, and putting their own children, and the legitimacy of the child protection system itself, at risk. The criminal justice system, a creaky, blundering vehicle for doing at least something about murders, thefts, and illicit drugs, itself ruins lives—even extinguishes them—in the name of justice. Shakespeare's Shylock could demand, within his rights, the enforcement of the contract calling for a pound of his opponent's flesh, but Shakespeare knew we would not call a system that enforced such a contract a just one. Too much justice can be injustice. Insatiable correction, retribution, and redistribution do not rectify or repair the world.

What would it take to feel poised beneath a suspended sword, engaged by the rigors of judgment and the outrage of injustice? We need practice cultivating the sense of injustice, experiencing and expressing the sense of outrage, and then exploring why. We need practice taking seeming misfortunes and finding the scope for human choice that justifies charges of injustice. We need practice seeing that there can be too much even of this, and learning to know when and where is it too much. Life affords enough unjust occasions, but practice requires some moral exercises.

6. PRACTICE

"Bugs die, but people don't, right, Mommy?" my four-year-old said. It wasn't really a question as much as an urgent need for reassurance I couldn't give. I started to say that people don't die unless they are very old, but I couldn't indulge even this small deceptive comfort. Too many interrupted lives come to mind.

Even if the fact of human mortality could be viewed as natural, fated, or tragic, early deaths, avoidable deaths, and murders invite perceptions of injustice. Yet because of their finality, because of the frozen grief they leave, many cruel deaths seem to defy even the righteous rage against injustice.

Three recent deaths preoccupy me. Each was a person cut off way too early, while vibrant, in living mid-sentence. One close friend was murdered, stabbed to death a block from her home while she took an early evening stroll to the convenience store. A long knife was found but no suspect. The vibrancy of Mary Joe Frug's life summoned hundreds of people to the memorial service. I learned there and since that her gifts for friendship, self-invention, and making each interlocutor feel uniquely important inspired even those who didn't know her to make more out of life.

The press periodically circles around the survivors, asking for developments in the criminal investigation and speculating, cruelly, about motives family members or friends might have had to destroy Mary Joe. That part feels like injustice to me. The murder itself feels so much worse than injustice, so unspeakable.

Then there is the failure of the criminal justice system to find a suspect or produce a trial. I notice this but feel no passion about it. It is not as if a suspect, a trial, even a conviction could do anything to bring back Mary Joe. Perhaps some sense of closure might come, but I doubt it, and I do not hope for closure nor for comprehension. If there were a trustworthy conviction, I might feel marginally more safe when I walk down the same street. There might be some small satisfaction from seeking consequences return to a brutal wrongdoer. But there is no way to correct or rectify what happened here. That her children thrive is some comfort; that they echo her while being very much themselves is, for me, some piece of justice.

Another murder happened shortly thereafter but received little of the same media attention. A teenager was killed in a revenge murder by another teen. I knew him slightly; he did some odd jobs for my neighbors and good friends who had befriended the boy's family, although they lived worlds away in an inner city neighborhood. My neighbors worked with Tom Roderick's mother in advocacy for welfare recipients, and the political friendship turned into almost extended family ties. My neighbors coached the Roderick kids for job interviews, helped the mother in her dealings with state bureaucracies, and listened when the gaps between their worlds made nothing else possible. Tom was getting himself together; he had withdrawn from the gang and had assumed responsibility for maintaining order in a five-block area around his home. When a child within the neighborhood was attacked by someone from another area, Tom meted out consequences and beat up an older relative of the offending kid. He was murdered, apparently, in a further stage of the cycle of revenge and threat that are fixtures in that particular urban culture. He was eighteen.

At the memorial service, people spoke of the foreshortened deaths of so many young people in that community, and of the racial, class, and gang world divisions deserving blame. United at the service were a rainbow of religious voices, a spectrum of Christian, Islamic, and Buddhist ones. A political leader spoke and said that in the room was the knowledge of what had happened; in the room was the capacity to bring justice out of tragedy if only the people who knew would tell the police.

Yes, some steps toward justice could emerge if those who knew would tell what happened, and real consequences were produced for the specific wrongdoers. But observers in the community said the "system" seemed irrelevant because it would only put away an offending youth for a few months before sending him back to the streets, older and more angry. How is this system of arrest, prosecution, and incarceration different than the informal neighborhood processes of retribution and vengeance, rotating through the cohort of teens? Each one wounded or dead in the streets, or locked up away from them, becomes another check in the column of "taken" in this nasty game, another trigger for the next move. Neighborhood watches escalate into gangs; gangs justify further armament and violence; the society justifies further prosecutions and prisons. Too much justice is no justice, especially when it looks like "just us," just African American males taking the hits.

Real justice, I think, lies in a different direction. Every one of the kids—the murder victim, the killer, the surrounding gang members—would get some real choices, some real schooling, some safe homes, some parents with enough time, resources, and self-worth to parent fully. The event, if it happened, would be rare enough to be news riveting the media rather than the commonplace story it became. And it wouldn't be just one household in my neighborhood in mourning, but all of them, all knowing our mutual implication in the lives of the next generation. For there to be something approximating justice, everyone with the ability to respond would feel and act with responsibility. This would not bring back one eager, handsome, earnest youngster, who meant so much to his family, and perhaps that is why justice seems so cold as well as distant.

And then, a third death. Another friend. She had cancer, breast cancer. She went through treatment. She prevailed. Until it came back. She researched all the options, and because she was Betsy Lehman, smart, curious, indefatigable—and a science writer for a leading newspaper—she found the best, cutting-edge program that would give her a real chance. The treatment regime she underwent stretched even her courage, effervescence, and will. When we heard she died, I felt shock because her confidence had been so infectious. She had put everything on the line to live for her husband and her two young girls.

We learned a few weeks later that actually the treatment had cleared her of cancer; she must have died from a stroke or other bodily response to the massive doses of chemotherapy. I struggled to find some way to locate this information. Is death just inevitable and not to be cheated? Groping for some such notion of the exigencies of bodies and their limits, Betsy's friends and family then received the next wave of shocking news. There had been a mistake in the treatment. Betsy had undergone four times the already enormous dose of chemotherapy as specified by the protocol. Somebody killed her with what could only be described as poison.

My anguish turned into fury. I remembered that Betsy had called a friend shortly before she died and left a message that something wasn't right. With horror, I realized she knew and tried to stop the human mistakes that killed her, but no one else knew in time. Internal and external investigations exposed not one, but more than half a dozen people at the distinguished Dana Farber Cancer Research Institute involved in the mistaken dosage over two days: the resident who wrote the amount in the chart, the pharmacists who released the dosage, the nurses who checked the chart and monitored the patient.[15] Investigations exposed the lack of internal controls to ensure proper dosage or monitor the quality of patient care in this world-renown center for cancer research and treatment. World-class research apparently had not required more than indifference to actual client care.

Indifference killed my friend, who could make perfect chocolate eclairs while explaining deftly the latest treatments of children's ear infections. She left her three- and six-year-old girls to grow up with a heartbroken father who struggles now also to be a mother. That the Dana Farber would treat any patient this way is intolerable. Any patient there would be willing to take the known risks to advance knowledge about cancer treatment, but why would any submit to human blunders? The researchers betrayed the trust of those putting their lives on the line to assist future patients as well as themselves. That the Dana Farber committed egregious mistakes on a science journalist indicated at least equal indifference if not utter stupidity; that Betsy happened to be married to a research scientist working at another part of the same institute revealed that no one could be ensured careful attention there.

Does a financial settlement for the family approach justice? No, though it eases the daily living with devastation. Is it justice when the student internist who wrote the wrong dosage and the pharmacists who filled it receive discipline? Only of the most superficial kind. Their errors were only the predictable mistakes of imperfect persons. The injustice that must be rectified is the systemic refusal to plan for and guard against those predictable mistakes. Something

---

15.   Richard A. Knox, "Dana-Farber Puts Focus on Mistakes in Overdose," *Boston Globe,* 31 October 1995, p. 1.

moves toward justice in the shake-up and reorganization of the Dana Farber to ensure double- and triple-checking whenever a dosage of chemical poisons exceeds specified safe levels. A step toward justice appeared in the national attention given to Betsy Lehman's death, a death due to correctable errors in clinical care and basic accounting methods available to guard against them. To seek justice here means: Put in place checks to prevent predictable human errors in the future. See human choices, not mere accidental mistakes and not acts of God, in even the death of a cancer patient.

Law and communal responses cannot restore the world marked by injustice, but only move some of the broken pieces around. Maybe we can limit injustices in the future. But only if we sharpen the sense of injustice. Life, and deaths, give us the occasions, continually. But perception of injustice in these occasions takes practice. We need to exercise the capacity to be outraged, the ability to sort out the inevitable from what could be different—to rework the inevitable into what could be different—and yet not to thirst for too much justice. We need the practice of telling and hearing stories. Try on the sensibilities of other acute observers of injustice, discern what moves you, and why. Test the sense of injustice, and seek east.

A GENETICS OF JUSTICE

My mother grew up in the Dominican Republic under the absolute dictatorship of el Generalísimo Rafael Leónidas Trujillo. Respectable families such as hers kept their young daughters out of the public eye, for Trujillo was known to have an appetite for pretty girls, and once his eye was caught, there was no refusing him.

Of course, my mother was intrigued and wanted to meet the great man. She knew nothing of the horrid crimes of the dictatorship, for her parents were afraid to say anything—even to their own children—against the regime. So, as a young girl of thirteen, my mother thought of el Jefe as a kind of movie star. He was her version of the long-haired rock and rollers on the *Ed Sullivan Show* her daughters screamed at almost three decades later.

But her only image of the dictator was the one that hung in every house next to the crucifix and la Virgencita with the gloss beneath: *In this house Trujillo is Chief.* The pale face of a young military man wearing a plumed bicorne hat and a gold-braided uniform looked down beneficently at my mother as she read her romantic novellas and dreamed of meeting the great love of her life. Sometimes in her daydreams, her great love wore the handsome young dictator's face. Never having seen him, my mother could not know the portrait was heavily touched up.

By the time my mother married my father, a revolutionary who had been forced into exile, she knew all about the true nature of the dictatorship. Thousands had lost their lives in failed attempts to return the country to democracy. Relations, whom she had assumed had dropped off as family friends, turned out to have disappeared. My father had been one of the lucky ones. He had narrowly escaped to Canada after the plot he had participated in as a student failed. That same year, 1937, el Generalísimo ordered the overnight slaughter of some twenty thousand Haitians, who had come across the border to work on sugar cane plantations for slave wages. It was from my father that my mother learned that Trujillo hated blacks with a vengeance and disguised his own Haitian ancestry by lightening his complexion with makeup. Now she understood why, years back, her family had had to hide Chucha in a trunk in Mamayaya's bedroom the night the guardia came by and why el Jefe had declared his nation officially white although everyone could look around and see that the truth was otherwise.

Perhaps because she had innocently revered him, my mother was now doubly revolted by this cold-blooded monster. He became something of an obsession with her—living as she was by then in exile with my father, isolated from her family who were still living on the island. As my sisters and I were growing up, many of my mother's cautionary stories figured Trujillo and his excesses.

Whenever we misbehaved, she would use his example as proof that character shows from the very beginning. One such story showed the seeds of Trujillo's megalomania. As a child, Trujillo insisted that his mother sew coke bottle tops or chapitas to his shirt front so that he could have a chest of medals. Later, the underground's code name for him would be Chapita because of his attachment to his hundreds of medals.

When my sisters and I cared too much about our appearance, my mother would tell us how Trujillo's vanity knew no bounds. How in order to appear taller, his shoes were specially made abroad with built-in heels that added inches to his height. How plumes for his Napoleonic hats were purchased in Paris and shipped in vacuum-packed boxes to the island. How his uniforms were trimmed with tassels and gold epaulettes and red sashes, pinned with his medals, crisscrossing his chest. How he costumed himself in dress uniforms and ceremonial hats and white gloves—all of this in a tropical country where men wore guayaberas in lieu of suit jackets, short-sleeved shirts worn untucked so the body could be ventilated. My mother could go on and on.

At this point I would always ask her why she and my father had returned to live in the country if they knew the dictatorship was so bad. And that's when my mother would tell me how under pressure from his friends up north, Trujillo pretended to be liberalizing his regime. How he invited all exiles back to form parties and partici-pate in the first free elections in two decades. My father had been pressured by his in-laws to return, only to discover that the liberal-ization was a hoax staged so that the regime could keep the good-will and dollars of the United States.

My father and mother were once again trapped in a police state. They laid low as best they could. Now that they had four young daughters, they could not take any chances. For a while anyhow, that spark of justice that had almost cost my father his life and that he had instilled in my mother seemed to have gone out. Periodi-cally, Trujillo would demand a tribute, and they would acquiesce. A tax, a dummy vote, a portrait on the wall. The most humiliating of these tributes to my father and other men in the country was the occasional parade in which the women were made to march alone and turn their heads and acknowledge the great man as they passed the review stand. If you did not march, your cédula would not be stamped, and without a stamped identification card, there was nothing you could do, including what my parents were petitioning to do: obtain passports to leave the country under the pretext that my father wanted to study heart surgery. There was no heart sur-geon in the country, he argued, and our dictator had been known to suffer chest pains. It was his patriotic duty, and so on.

The time came when my mother had to march. The parade went on for hours in the hot sun until my mother was sure she was going to faint. Her feet were swollen and hurting. The back of her dress was damp with sweat. Finally, when she thought she could not go one more step, there was the grandstand in sight, a clutter of dress uni-forms, a vague figure on the podium. Suddenly, the parade stopped as my mother walked into el Jefe's line of vision. Somebody ahead had fainted, and the orderlies were rushing forward with their stretcher to resuscitate the woman in question. Under her breath, my mother was cursing this monster who would drag thousands of women out on the hot streets to venerate him. She looked up at him, and what she saw made her smile with glee.

No more than ten steps away stood a short, plump man sweating profusely in his heavy dress uniform. The medals on his chest flashed brightly with the hot sun beaming down on them so that he looked as if he had caught on fire. Under his Napoleonic hat, she could see the rivulets of sweat, and his pancake makeup running down his face revealed his dark, tanned skin beneath. My mother said that as she stood there, el Jefe seemed to be coming undone. Then the line moved on, and my mother marched out of sight. It was the one and only time that my mother saw the man who had ruled her imagination most of her life.

My mother and father got their passports in August 1960, and twenty-four hours later we were on a plane headed for New York. Nine months after our departure, on May 30, 1961, the group of plotters with whom my father had been associated assassinated the dictator. Actually, Dominicans do not refer to the death as an assassination but as an *ajusticiamiento*, a bringing to justice. Finally, after thirty-one years, Trujillo was brought to justice, found guilty, and executed.

But the execution was an external event, not necessarily an internal exorcism. All their lives my parents, along with a nation of Dominicans, had learned the habits of repression, censorship, terror. These would not disappear with a few bullets and a national liberation proclamation. These would also not disappear with a plane ride north and hundreds of miles distance between the island and our apartment in New York.

And so, long after we had left, my parents were still living in the dictatorship inside their own heads. Even on American soil, they were afraid of awful consequences if they spoke out or disagreed with authorities. The First Amendment right to free speech meant nothing to them. Silence about anything "political" was the rule in our house.

In fact, my parents rarely spoke about the circumstances of our leaving the island. To us, their daughters, they offered the official story: My father had come to study heart surgery. We were not told that our house had been surrounded every night by the black Volkswagens of the SIM, the secret police; that my father had been on the verge of being arrested; that we had finally escaped to the United States. But this great country that had offered my parents a refuge had also created the circumstances that made them have to seek a refuge in the first place. It was this same United States that had helped put our dictator in place during its occupation of the country from 1916–1924. As Secretary of State Cordell Hull had said, Trujillo is an SOB but at least he's our SOB. But about all these matters, my parents were silent, afraid that ungratefulness would result in our being sent back to where we came from.

My mother especially lived in terror of the consequences of living as free citizens. In New York City, Dominican exiles gathered around the young revolutionary Bosch planning an invasion of the island. Every time my father attended these meetings, my mother would get tragic about the danger he was putting his family in again. If Americans found out he was politicking against "their dictator," they might deport us. If the Dominican SIM found out about my father's activities, family members remaining behind were likely to be in danger. Even our own family in New York could suffer consequences. Five years earlier, in 1955, Galindez, an expatriate anti-Trujillo professor teaching at Columbia University, had disappeared from a New York subway. The same thing could happen to us.

I don't know if my father complied with my mother's entreaties or just got so busy trying to make a living in this country. But after a few months of hotheaded attendance, he dropped out of these political activities and his silence deepened. During my early teen years in this country, I knew very little about what was actually going on in the Dominican Republic. Whenever la situación on the island came up, my parents spoke in hushed voices. In November 1960, four months after our arrival, when *Time* magazine reported the murder of the three Mirabal sisters, who along with their husbands had started the national underground in the Dominican Republic, my parents confiscated the magazine. To our many questions about what was going on, my mother always had the ready answer, "En boca cerrada no entran moscas." No flies fly into a closed mouth. Later, I found out that this very saying had been written above the entrance of the SIM's torture center at La Cuarenta.

Given this mandate of silence, I was a real thorn in my mother's side.

———

She had named me, her second of four daughters, after herself, so we shared the same name. Of all her babies, she reports, I was the best behaved until I learned to talk. Then, I would not shut up. I always had to answer her back when I disagreed with her. Childhood was rocky, but adolescence was a full-fledged war.

Still, my mother found ways of controlling me. The Trujillo cautionary tales worked momentarily in that I loved to hear those outlandish stories. Her threats to throw me off as her daughter for being disrespectful were more effective. And disrespect—as she had learned in the dictatorship—was anything short of worship. When Eleanor Roosevelt's grandson published a biography of his famous grandmother, my mother said he should be ashamed of himself (*meglamona*) for calling his grandmother "a plain woman."

"But she was a plain woman," I argued. "That's just saying the truth."

"Truth! What about honoring his grandmother?" My mother's eyes had that look she saw in my eyes when she said, "If looks could kill . . . "

Unfortunately for my mother, I grew up to be a writer who published under my maiden name, which was also her name. At first my mother flushed with personal pride when friends mistook her for the writer. "The poem in your Christmas card was so beautiful! You're quite the poet, Julia!" But after I became a published writer, friends who had read a story or an essay of mine in some journal would call up and say, "Wow, I didn't know you were such a feminist!" My mother had no idea what ideas she was being thought responsible for. When I published a first novel with a strong autobiographical base, she did not talk to me for months.

When I started to work on my second novel, the trouble started up again. She had heard from one of my sisters that I was writing about the dictatorship. The novel would be a fictional retelling of the story of three sister freedom fighters, contemporaries of my mother, whose murders had been reported in that confiscated *Time* magazine. This time, my mother warned, I was not just going to anger family members, but I would be directly responsible for their lives. There were still old cronies of the dictator around who would love an excuse to go after my family, after my father, after her.

This was one of the hardest challenges I had ever had to face as a writer. If my mother were indeed speaking the truth, could I really put my work above the lives of human beings? But if I shut up, wouldn't I still be fanning the embers of the dictatorship with its continuing power of censorship and control over the imagination of many Dominicans? I talked to my cousins in the Dominican Republic and asked them if my mother's dire predictions had any foundation. They shook their heads. "The old people still see a SIM agent under every bush!" they explained.

When the novel came out, I decided to send it to her. I dedicated a copy to both my father and mother. In the accompanying note, I thanked them for having instilled in me through their sufferings my desire for justice and freedom. I mailed the package and then did what I seldom do except in those moments when I need all the help I can get—I made the sign of the cross as I exited the post office. Days later, my mother called me up to tell me she had just finished the novel. "You put me right back in those horrible days, and it was like I was reliving it all," she said, sobbing. "I don't care what happens to us! I'm so proud of you for writing this book."

I stood in my kitchen in Vermont stunned, relishing her praise and listening to her cry. It was one of the few times since I had learned to talk that I did not try to answer my mother back. If there is such a thing as genetic justice that courses through the generations and finally manifests itself full blown in a family moment, there it was.

A CONFESSION

1958, 1959. I was thirteen. And then fourteen. Heroes: Lou Gehrig and Babe Ruth among the dead. And Ernie Pyle, believe it or not, whose book, *Brave Men,* my father had given me to read. Among the living: Ted Williams, Roy Seivers, Willie Mays, Hank Aaron, Ernie Banks, Mickey Mantle. Floyd Patterson, who was then the youngest heavyweight champ in history. On the sky-blue bulletin board above my bunk there were pictures of his knockout of Archie Moore, the man he beat to take Rocky Marciano's vacated championship, back in 1956. I had rooted for him and felt low for him when he lost the title in that seven-knockdown debacle against the Swede, Ingemar Johanson. And in the summer of 1959 I had spent hours in the Viers Mill Theater on a Saturday afternoon (it was only a quarter then, and you could sit there all day) watching him knock Johanson out in five rounds of controlled fury, doing what Dempsey and Louis and all the others hadn't been able to do: win back the heavyweight championship. For weeks I had replayed the fight, shadowboxing alone in my room.

Then, the black athletes I admired were separated from me by their athletic skill and their age, more than anything else. And yet I lived in this strangely, tragically divided country, and there was a world outside the happy house where we were growing up. The kids I moved with every day in the neighborhood were all white, and they had two words they sometimes used when calling names: jew-boy and nigger.

These words were casually spoken. They seemed to be an attempt to abrade their target for some difference—never actual as far as I knew—beyond their control. Because I was an identical twin, with bright red hair and a very slight build, who had been called names pointing to my own particular differences or attributes (carrot top, skinny, rail, freckle-face), who had stood under the frank scrutiny of strangers and had felt singled out, freakish, even though my twin, Bobby, looked exactly like me—because I knew how uncomfortable these kinds of things made me feel, I refrained from the use of the words. This was visceral; at least I do not remember making a conscious decision about it. There was no high-mindedness in it either; it was closer to timidity and self-preservation than consideration for anyone else's feelings.

There was, of course, another class of words that the boys I knew used with great variety and regularity: those numberless combinations of expressions connected to sexuality, body parts, bodily functions, and privy acts. Everybody knows the words I'm talking about. In 1959 they carried a lot more weight than they do today, as movies and even television continue to give themselves over to a "realism" that insists on most of them, almost all the time. When I tell my young students that Jack Paar left the Tonight show because the network censored the use of the word "watercloset" on the air, they are usually incredulous. But that was how it was.

I had had it drummed into me in religion classes that the use of these—well, I'll call them classic—dirty words was a sin. We had all had it described for us in detail what hell was like: the fire that never stops and never consumes, the loss of the presence of God, the magnitude of what eternal burning meant ("If you take a stone as large as the earth, and every million years an eagle comes by and brushes its wing against the surface, in the time it would take that stone to wear away to nothing, Eternity would be only beginning").

And it seemed that all of our lessons were about a just, but severe God, attending most vigorously to all the sins of the flesh—

especially sins of the flesh. In our lessons, the seven deadly sins all came from the flesh—if it was pride, it was pride in the flesh; gluttony was flesh stuffing itself; sloth was flesh putrefying in laziness; envy was flesh wanting more than it could rightly have; greed was flesh; wrath was flesh. And flesh, in the alchemy of the time, meant sex. Somehow, that was what was always communicated. In every single instance, the message was that the sinful words were the ones about sexuality and body function. I do not know what people thought or what they might have meant to accomplish in those days, but that was what was communicated. Words like "jewboy" and "nigger" were not on the list of proscribed expressions—that is, they were not made clear as being sins. Perhaps they would not have been appreciated or encouraged; but they were considered impolite at best. And everyone understood this, mostly because of the weight of attention given to the words that contributed to the so-called prurient interest.

None of the Ten Commandments said anything about using words that take away a person's dignity. The commandment was *Thou shalt not curse.* Now, none of the bad words I have mentioned here were ever used in our house, and all of them were used wherever else I went. And I used them—the dirty ones.

Certainly there was more occasion for using them among the boys I moved with. There were several instances where I made efforts to refrain, and people wondered aloud what was wrong with me. I remember one boy particularly, who, for my benefit and in the company of other boys, spit into the creek where we were sitting and said, "Aw fuckshit, I mean, gosh," looking at me with a derisive, ironic smile.

So I fell into the use of the dirty words, though at the time I believed that to do so was to put myself at risk of spending eternity in hell. The idea of Justice for us then was that it stemmed from Divinity. It was couched in phrases of Divine anger ("Depart from me ye cursed!") and the punishments for those who incurred it. I was devout, but I was also just cowardly enough not to want to seem so different from the boys in whose company I found myself every day.

That is, I did not want to seem more exotic than I already was.

Obviously there's not much to recommend this rather timid boy, scared of the wrath of judgment, wanting to talk tough, wanting to seem like the others, painfully aware every day of what separates him and other boys—not just in his appearance and in the fact that he is an identical twin, but in the mental and spiritual baggage that he is carrying. A boy who cannot stop thinking about *consequences,* who is unable to simply be in-the-moment, like the boys he admires or of whom he is frightened. And withal, carrying around in his heart the sense of an imperious God, the justice that would crush him if he were unlucky enough to be snatched away by death before he could make his confession, his act of contrition.

I suppose a lot of Catholic boys were carrying some of this baggage in 1959.

Indeed, when I look back on it, the whole time seems weirdly suffused with a concentrated effort by every person in public authority—teachers, priests, nuns, senators & congressmen, the voices we heard on the radio, the people we saw on television—to control and somehow dampen the force of sexual energy that was making itself felt in the country. Example: rock n' roll, that proscribed music, exemplified by Elvis Presley's sideburns and swiveling hips and Chuck Berry's gymnastic stunts with the guitar. Example: the newer, steamier movies, with their suggestiveness and their portrayals of people whose lives were governed by unacceptable passions.

That year, the year just after Sputnik, with the increasing talk of the missile gap, the increasing worry over the Russians, I heard one of the boys at lunch say, "I'm gonna study Russian so when those bastards conquer us I'll know what they're talking about." This struck me funny. And like almost everything else that has ever struck me funny, I had an immediate urge to repeat it. The next morning, a Saturday, I was playing basketball with a friend, a young black man named John.

Now, I have to stop here to tell you a little something about John. I had known him for a few months. Though he was almost twenty-five, eleven years older than I was, we got along fine. I could make him laugh doing the voices of my teachers. He had stories about what he had seen overseas when he was stationed in Germany with the air force. He worked at the recreation center near the church where I spent afternoons and weekend days playing basketball. We drank cold cokes together, sitting on the porch rail and watching the shade change out on the basketball court. I remember once saying, in the perfect confidence of its truth, that it was probably God's will that people began to pick up an interest in the things for which they had a given talent. And I remember that he said, "That's not really a thing I'd expect a boy your age to say."

I felt very impressed with myself; he was an older man, a grown-up, and he seemed to approve. He did not use dirty language, and I could therefore keep from using it myself. So I could relax around him. I had begun to think of my time at the park in terms of whether he would be there, and when I'd see him, I'd wave. I would be out on the court shooting alone, the ball dropping through the chain net or bouncing off into the shady grass, the sound echoing into the surrounding trees. He would be a shadow on the big porch of the recreation center, wielding his broom or moving the metal chairs against the wall in the aftermath of one county recreational function or another, and he would stop and watch me. He'd said he liked watching me because I was a dead shot (his phrase), especially from the corner. I was proud to have his praise, again because he was a grown-up and had been out and around in the world. Now and then he would even take a break from his duties and come out and shoot a few with me. Usually this was in the few minutes before he headed home. Sometimes we played on into the dusk, talking about sports or about our families, about growing up. Sometimes we talked about Jesus, the stories of the New Testament, and the resurrection. We had wondered about the satellite hurtling across the sky beyond the reach of our vision.

John was very wide, stocky and muscular, with broad shoulders and large hands, a very powerful and yet rather uncoordinated man. He had never played a lot of basketball; but he enjoyed shooting around, and there were times when he would hit three or

four in a row, the ball coming in a nearly arcless path and banging
into the hole. The custom was then, and is now I think, to give
what is called "change" to the man who hits the bucket. You toss
him the ball and give him another shot. John would do this for
me, and I would do it for him. One afternoon I hit about fourteen
straight, and he took the ball and walked, dribbling slowly to the
other end of the court, then turned and stood there, smiling. "You
mind if I just hold it awhile?" I laughed deep, and he came back
dribbling and passed it to me, and I missed a layup, and we
laughed again.

When I'd leave, I'd call good-bye to him, walking up through
the woods, the shortcut that led to my neighborhood. I'd hear him
start his car and move off. If it had begun to rain, he would offer to
drive me home. The radio would be on, low. Jazz. He'd tap the
wheel to the music, and we wouldn't say much. "Thanks," I'd say,
when we'd pull in front of my house. "See you later," he'd say. I
don't recall that I ever asked him in, and yet I think if he had been
closer to my age I would have.

At any rate, this particular Saturday morning is his last morning
in this job; he's got a better opportunity in the city, and he's going
to start night school. He's interested in philosophy, thinks he might
want to become a minister someday. It's a sunny, breezy morning,
cool and fresh, and full of the promise of summer. He's finished the
last of his tasks and has come out to shoot some baskets; we're playing a last game of "horse" and talking about the most recent failure
of an American rocket to get off the ground. I remember the line I
heard the day before in the student cafeteria at school. "When I
grow up, I'm gonna study Russian so when those bastards conquer
us I'll know what they're talking about." On impulse, I begin to repeat it to John, wanting to make him laugh. But I am in the shadow
of my church, just up the hill on the other side of the trees, and I do
not want to utter the word "bastard" because it is a bad word—a
sin, this word. And it is not a word John uses, either.

So I edit myself.

The phrase needs some characterizing word to make it funny, a
word that characterizes the troublesome Russians; "bastards" is

funny, and I need some collective-sounding equivalent. So I end up using the word that in the society in which I live is the acceptable one, the one whose use would not cause me to be in jeopardy of losing my soul.

I say, "I'm gonna study Russian so when those niggers conquer us I'll know what they're talking about." For an instant I am glad of myself because, as I said, John doesn't use dirty words.

A full five seconds goes by before it dawns on me what I have done.

He moves across the key at about the foul line, dribbling the ball, then just stops. For an instant, it's as if the energy has simply gone out of him—the very animation of being alive there opposite me in the brightness. I think now it must have been the most profound discouragement. "Well," he says, after a terrible pause, "guess I better get on home now."

I will never forget the look on his face.

In a movie of roughly that time called *Calamity Jane,* starring Doris Day, there's a passage where, as Calamity Jane, she is shooting at Indians who are chasing a stage coach she's riding on. She screams, "Come on, you Redskin nigger heathens." When I ask people who saw the movie in 1957 if they remember this line, they have no memory of it. Had the scriptwriter provided another phrase for her, and the censors, by some strange quirk or oversight, had let it through, so that her line was, "Come on, you motherfucking sons of bitches!" it of course would have caused a tremendous stir.

Even later—twenty years later—when the TV networks aired the movie *The Sting* the first time, they edited out the word "crap" and left in the word "nigger." And when this article was under consideration by the *New York Times Magazine,* the editor there informed me that the rule still applies: I could use the word "nigger" in this article, but not the others; I would have to characterize them, somehow. So you see we are still operating under the same terrible inconsistency.

Roughly ten years after that afternoon at the recreation center, I happened upon a photograph that has never left me; it still has the power to terrify me. The war in Vietnam had heated up, and I had

enlisted in the air force. I was stationed at Chanute Air Force Base,
Illinois. It was a breezy, early spring day, most of which I had spent
alone in my barracks room. Outside the window, birds sang, tree-
shade moved, and friends were dying on the other side of the world.
The cities were burning. Martin Luther King was dead. Robert
Kennedy was dead. I had been looking through one of those big *Life*
magazine picture books—something a roommate had brought in,
filled with riveting photographs. For at least a couple of years now
I had been wondering if I might be a writer. The pictures had begun
to whisper stories to me: There was the famous shot of the sailor
kissing the woman on the street in New York the day World War II
ended. There was the burning Hindenburg. There were pictures of
bombed out buildings, the ravages of war. And there was the one I
am remembering now, with a chill.

I gazed at it for several seconds before I understood what it was:
a group of people standing in a small half-circle, looking for all the
world as though this is a festive occasion—a baking contest at a
state fair or a square dance. Men and women and one small girl in a
white dress, no more than eight or nine years old. Smiles on the
faces, especially the little girl's face. It's a party. Everyone is happy.
And there, suspended in the middle of them, is the object of their
obvious pleasure in the moment: the body of a hanged black man,
from the look of it no more than a teenager, his smooth face curi-
ously passive, the rope cutting deep into the flesh of his neck, the
body so profoundly heavy, drooping, the feet only inches from the
ground. Every face but his is perfectly satisfied, and there is no trace
of horror, or anger, or reluctance, or any human emotion that you
might ordinarily attach to the terror, the appalling fact, of a man's
death on a summer afternoon. These are clear consciences. Justice
has been done. I remember that the picture was said to have been
taken at a lynching in the 1930s, and so this is before the Germans
and the Austrians and the East Europeans had developed the newer,
faster ways to dispense that kind of justice.

I believe that it is at least possible that the same thing that
makes it acceptable to print the ethnic slur and not the so-called ob-
scenity is present in the fact that a little girl can attend to the death

of a man with such calm. Justice had been done. In the minds of these people, clearly, something has been preserved, and society is again protected from all the bugaboos that threaten it.

It is a lynching, a murder for which no one will be punished.

Couple this with the fact that when Rosa Parks refused to move to the back of that bus in Alabama, back in 1954, she was *breaking the law*.

One needn't look at these two things very long before it becomes clear that law is a frail human concept, an agreement, slowly or carelessly or fearfully arrived at, to protect human expectations. And, of course, it contains violent and dreadful inconsistencies. Exactly as society does.

I hope I have been raising my children to be aware of those inconsistencies. I understand, of course, that the world they move in outside my house communicates other things to them. This is a strangely retrograde time, with groups rushing to define themselves and other groups by abstractions, with hate being held up as some God-given right or even as a sort of weird heritage, a redress for grievances old and new, or a pretext to barricade one's self up in a cabin in Montana.

Hate kills everything it touches. No matter where it comes from or what its reasons are, it makes people less than they could be. I still hope that this country—the one with the word "happiness" in the preamble to its constitution—might, as Martin Luther King once said, finally live up to its promise. When my three older children were younger, I actually had moments of thinking that it might be on its way to doing just that: becoming a place where people see each other *one at a time*. Certainly that is worth struggling for, through disappointment and hurt and all the rest.

I should have been able to say something to John. I should have been able to apologize. In my mind, it was not uttering the offending word, finally, but failing to walk over to my friend and tell him what an idiot I was for making such a mistake—that was the first racist act I ever committed. I hope with all my heart it was the last.

I remember that I was paralyzed with embarrassment and unable to think of a single word to utter. Me, the boy who was supposed to be so good with words.

He walked off, got in his car and drove away, and I never saw him again.

TRUE MORALITY

My friend and I were taking a walk one summer day in Port-au-Prince, and in the late afternoon we stopped for a beer at a small establishment called Le Bar Sportif. There was just room in the little concrete porch for a table and the two chairs we sat in. Presently the brother of the proprietor appeared and engaged us in conversation. He was un homme de couleur (to judge from his coppery skin tone) elegantly dressed in a three-piece suit (he seemed perfectly comfortable in this garb, despite the crushing heat), and proved to be a lawyer. It was chiefly my friend who supported the talk, for I was exhausted by culture shock and the effort of functioning in my rudimentary French.

My friend is the son of a European lawyer, and he and the Haitian attorney were soon deep in a discussion of the Code Napoléon. The conversation went on for a couple of hours, during which the evening thunderstorm began with great force. Seeing that we were trapped, the Haitian lawyer went out and borrowed a car from an acquaintance so he could drive us back to where we were staying; we invited him into the hotel bar and went on talking there for a time.

My vocabulary was insufficient to follow the discussion completely; I drifted in and out. But at one point there occurred a phrase that caught my ear. The Haitian lawyer made a significant pause before pronouncing it with a flourish, as though it were some ultimate trump card he'd produced from the vest of his good-looking suit: *"La vraie morale se moque de la morale."* At this, my friend grunted and dropped his head, as if to acknowledge that he had indeed been trumped.

My father also practiced as a lawyer for many years and currently serves as a circuit court judge, traveling among four rural counties of middle Tennessee. I tried the line on him when I got back to the States. I found it a little difficult to translate, but a literal rendition might be this: "True morality makes a mockery of all morality."

My father thought it over for a little more than a moment. He seemed to be struck, as I had been, by the conceptual peculiarity of the statement. Presently he shrugged and said that probably someone should tell Pat Robertson that—Robertson and all the other self-proclaimed guardians of morals who have been infesting our country of late. From that reply I took it that he'd understood the sentence in much the same way I had.

One of the things that interested me is that while my father and I found this sentence to be unusual and striking, whenever I try it on people of French culture they take it entirely as a matter of course. Later on I trotted it out in Paris at a dinner party of French publishing people; all were familiar with the source (Montesquieu[1]) and all had a ready interpretation. It seemed to me that both the line and its implications were so well known to these people, who had apparently grown up knowing all about them, that it had lost its capacity to puzzle or surprise. It had become in effect invisible within its familiarity . . . as touchstones of our own sense of justice such as "We hold these truths to be self-evident, that all men are created equal, that they are endowed by their Creator with certain unalienable Rights, that among these are Life, Liberty and the pursuit of Happiness" have become invisibly familiar to us in the United States.

La vraie morale se moque de la morale. The sentence was entirely new to me that Haitian evening, and when I first heard it, it seemed

---

1. Or so I was told, on more than one occasion. My quest for an exact citation, however, led to a rather different result; see below.

to have a ring of unexpected truth. It still feels true to me, as I think it would to most auditors educated in the American traditions. One reflexively tends to accept the proposition that *true morality* is infinitely and obviously superior to whatever moralizing systems may be put forward on false or limited premises. What one *knows to be right* is the ultimate standard of judgment—but where and how is *la vraie morale* to be identified? It seems to me that there is no simple answer to this question.

In *L'Ésprit des Lois,* Montesquieu derives the concept of natural law from God. *"Dieu a du rapport avec l'univers comme créateur et comme conservateur; les lois selon lesquelles il a créé sont celles selon lesquelles il conserve: il agit selon ses règles, parce qu'il les connaît; il les connaît parce qu'il les a faites; il les a faites parce qu'elles ont du rapport avec sa sagesse et sa puissance."*[2] This sentence (like the line *la vraie morale se moque de la morale)* has a noticeable flavor of tautology, but God is commonly allowed to be tautological; consider God's Old Testament self-definition: *I am that I am.* According to Montesquieu, axiomatic principles of justice can ultimately be referred, as above, to the wisdom and power of God: *"Avant qu'ils eût des lois faites, il y avait des rapports de justice possibles, et par conséquent des lois possibles. Dire qu'il n'y a rien de juste ni d'injuste que ce qu'ordonnent ou défendent les lois positives, c'est dire qu'avant qu'on eût tracé de cercle, tous les rayons n'étaient pas égaux."*[3]

According to this construction, justice as an absolute exists prior to whatever "positive laws" might be encoded to support and enforce it. In the same sense, *la vraie morale* presumably exists (as a sort of Platonic ideal) prior to any codified moral systems devised to promulgate it. And one would suppose that, in both cases, the latter must be checked against the former from time to time.

2.   God relates to the universe both as creator and as conservator; the laws of his creation are also those of his conservation: He acts according to his rules because he knows them; he knows them because they are of his own making; he made them because they are related to his wisdom and his power. Montesquieu, *L'Ésprit des Lois* (Paris, 1892) 6.

3.   Before any laws were made, there existed possible relations of justice, and by consequence there existed potential laws. To say that here is nothing just or unjust other than what is ordered or forbidden by positive laws is like saying that before a circle has been traced, all its radii are not equal. Montesquieu, *L'Ésprit,* 6.

The ultimate source of absolute justice is to be found, by this reasoning, in the wisdom and power of God. Thus verifying *la vraie morale* remains a sufficiently simple matter so long as God is present to remind us what it is. Such was still the case for Montesquieu (though he did feel the need, in the first chapter of *L'Ésprit des Lois,* to mount an argument against atheism), but such is no longer the case for us.

Of course, there are plenty of people in the United States who still live by faith, but notwithstanding all the ranting and raving of the Christian Right, the links between our legal system and any religiously based morality have been almost completely severed—a situation that is, after all, the subject of most of that same ranting and raving. My guess would be, however, that among most practitioners of law in this country this noise is heard as mere static. Members of the bar are almost always educated persons, and nowadays such persons, if they have not been educated out of their religion altogether, have most likely learned to keep their religion at a clean remove from the practical exigencies of life in the temporal world. For example, my Father, who rises so early in the morning that he cannot stay up very late at night, found it necessary a few years ago to begin videotaping the television show *L.A. Law* so he could watch fragments of it over his predawn coffee; he was interested in the program not for its entertainment value but because he had discovered that it was powerfully instrumental in forming the self-conception of many of the young lawyers who appeared in his court. This phenomenon was mysterious to him, and he felt a need to study and try to understand it.

Among the educated classes in this country today, the most popular source of spiritual solace is not Islam or Buddhism or Judaism or Christianity in any of its forms; instead it is psychotherapy. I think it is fair to generalize that the goal of psychotherapy in all or most of its manifestations is individual happiness—the same state that the Declaration of Independence promises us all the right to pursue. But two-hundred-odd years after the age of both Montesquieu and Jefferson, this pursuit has perhaps turned out to be a little isolating. If psychotherapy substitutes for religion, then we live in conditions of *chacun pour soi*—every man for himself—and isn't this the Hobbesian universe? Certainly it is the world portrayed by *L.A. Law.* Under such conditions, justice becomes *what's right for me.*

La vraie morale se moque de la morale. When tautologies have their ultimate source in the divine, there is not much use in challenging them, as we may learn (among other exercises) by reading the Book of Job. But when tautologies are not supported and underwritten by the wisdom and power of God, they may bear some looking into. If I use myself as an example, I would say that most people do have an internal sense of justice that *feels* innate to them: an inner wellspring of *la vraie morale.* But if God didn't put it in there (like some sort of spiritual hardwiring), two questions arise: Where did it come from? Is it the same as everybody else's?

The self-evidence of fundamental principles of justice tends to be taken for granted, yet such an assumption is not by any means safe. Consider that, before the three revolutions that ended the eighteenth century and laid the foundation of the modern world, "unalienable rights" to "Life, Liberty and the pursuit of Happiness" had not been taken to be self-evident for anyone, even for white people. What had been self-evident up until that point in history were principles such as the divine right of kings. In fact, the idea of natural human rights to freedom and self-determination was so extraordinarily novel in those days that it was necessary to fight revolutionary wars to assert it—to defeat people and parties whose (innate?) sense of justice told them something very different about what was right.

Both the American and the French Revolutions were founded on the concept of natural human rights, but neither of these revolutions ever intended to include any niggers in their various declarations of the rights of man. In the third revolution of this revolutionary age, which took place in Haiti, the niggers decided to include themselves, and in so doing ceased to be niggers at all and instead became free men and women. The black people of Haiti even became, for a brief period, French citizens, though eventually it seemed better to them to get rid of the French (who were determined to restore slavery in their possessions) and live instead as Haitian citizens. Thus it seems reasonable to say that of the three great revolutions of the eighteenth century, only the Haitian Revolution carried the ideology of natural human rights to its complete consummation.

The exclusion of African slaves (and, of course, American Indians too) from the doctrine of natural human rights proclaimed by the American Revolution cannot but seem a very significant and even hypocritical omission from the twentieth-century perspective. Preposterous, isn't it, that a society founded on the idea of human rights to freedom could maintain a slavery system for the first century of its existence? Indeed we know that the persistence of slavery was a tortured question for several of the country's founders, and we also know that all of them went to their graves without doing anything effective to resolve that question.

From our perspective it now seems self-evident that the persistence of slavery in new-founded United States amounted to a crack in the foundation of our nation, and that because this fault line has never fully healed it continues to send tremors through the fabric of our society today. It is possible, however, that the monumental injustice of slavery was *not* self-evident to free American citizens who lived during slavery time—that instead of being a contradiction of that inner sense of true morality, the existence of slavery was perfectly consonant with a private recognition of *la vraie morale*. For instance, there was the "Christian" proposition that the slavery system amounted to a massive effort to convert the heathen Africans and bring them to the way, the truth, and the light of righteous religion. More radical still was the idea that black African people were not in fact human beings, in which case there was no problem whatsoever in excluding them from the human rights enjoyed by white Europeans. Such arguments were put forward by an eighteenth-century Frenchman named Panon (for want of a better word he may be called, I suppose, an anthropologist) who wrote, in all scientific seriousness, "*J'assimile le nègre ni au singe, ni à l'homme Eu-ropéen.*"[4] For better or worse it seems clear that such statements could not have inspired in Panon's audience the instinctive moral repugnance that they would in most of us today.

One is forced to the conclusion that the revolutions of the eigh-teenth century were fought not only over the definition of human rights but over who, in the final analysis, is defined to *be* a human being. This question, though often unvoiced, has always underlain the problem of defining the status of people of mixed European and African blood. In the French slave societies, *les sang-mêlés* were al-ways considered to be a breed apart from either Europeans or Africans; whether such colored people were free or slave depended on the good or ill will of their European parents, but either way they were understood to belong to a separate race. This French view of the situation persists in Haiti (and to some extent, in Louisiana, because of the French influence there). In the American slavery sys-tem, however, this choice was always defined to be *black and white:* As little as one-sixteenth part of black blood was sufficient to turn someone from a self-determining human being into a piece of prop-erty. In American society today, a drop of black blood (if acknowl-edged) makes one altogether black. Only very recently have Amer-icans of mixed European and African blood begun to argue for such recognitions as a separate census category; whether such initiatives will have any effect on the racial caste system in today's United States remains to be seen.

The French system (which in prerevolutionary Haiti included sixty-four distinct shades of interbreeding, each with a name and predefined social status) certainly seems more accurate than the American; as to which is more *just,* the question seems moot. And if nowadays these two different systems have only to do with deter-mining degrees of skin tone, we should remember that in former times these systems were responsible for defining degrees of hu-manity. When I (and you too, I hope) look at a person of whatever color, I instinctively and immediately recognize a fellow human

4.   I categorize the Negro neither with the monkeys, nor with European men.

being; when our fellow citizens of bygone times looked at the same person, it was quite possible for them to instinctively and immediately recognize a two-legged beast of burden. The inner moral compass, located in the same interior redoubt for me as for my slave-owning ancestor, points to opposite conclusions in our two different cases.[5]

For white people, examples from the other side of the racial divide may be more illuminating.

On that same visit to Haiti when I first heard Montesquieu's interesting remark on true morality, I also interviewed a musician named Theodore Beaubrûn, who is a member of a popular group called Boukman Eksperyans. This band is perhaps the best-known example of a movement in Haitian popular music called *la musique des racines*,[6] which appropriates its rhythms from vaudou ceremonies. Vaudou has been heavily influential in Haitian politics since the time of the revolution, and *la musique des racines* extends this influence into song lyrics. The lyrics of Boukman Eksperyans have enough political significance that members of the band have received serious and credible death threats from the opposition.

I was curious as to why this band had chosen to associate itself with Boukman, a vaudou priest who in 1791 presided over a ceremony at Bois Cayman; on this occasion the slave insurrection that would become the first act of the Haitian Revolution was planned. From my point of view, Boukman's chief claim to fame was that he was there at the beginning. He was not a very effective military strategist, he got himself killed rather early in the struggle, and he also led a great many of his comrades to deaths that might have been avoided. I chiefly associated the ceremony at Bois Cayman with the plan to massacre all the whites living on Haiti's northern plain, a plan that was soon carried out with very considerable success.

5. I should say that I intend no aspersion against the South. The South is my country, though I have always lived in exile from it, due to events that took place long before I was born. I love my country, but still there are aspects of its tradition I would prefer to reform than defend.
6. Roots music.

It quickly became clear that Theodore Beaubrûn had a very different notion. In his scheme of things, the ceremony at Bois Cayman seemed to hold a place similar to that of the Sermon on the Mount in ours. (Most black Haitians seem to feel much the same; Bois Cayman is perhaps the single most significant date in the vaudou calendar.) For Beaubrûn, the unique importance of Boukman resides in the fact that he created for the first time a sense of national Haitian unity, drawing Africans of widely different tribal origin into a sense of solidarity defined by both the vaudou religion and the Creole language. That this union was soon to be cemented by the blood of slaughtered white people was *not* especially important to his view of the event. The massacre of the whites was peripheral, incidental, to the true meaning of the ceremony at Bois Cayman; it was an essentially trivial issue. They were only white people, after all.

I can see both sides of this issue now, but it requires a certain conscious effort. And the fact remains that my first instinctive response to Bois Cayman (though typical for white Americans, I've learned from inquiry) is 180 degrees opposite to the response of the average black Haitian. Again, our internal moral compasses are found to be pointing in very different directions.

Let us carry the point closer to home. I think the split reaction to the acquittal of O. J. Simpson will be remembered for a long time as one of the most disturbing seismic events to stem from the racial fault running through the foundation of our society in the United States. Prior to the Simpson acquittal, it had been a long time since we had had such a compelling example of total mutual incomprehension between black and white Americans. I think I find myself somewhere near the middle on this issue (if any middle ground remains), but still I was astonished to see film and photographs of black Americans reacting to news of Simpson's acquittal not with subtle smiles of gratified cynicism (as I might have done myself), but by literally jumping up in the air for joy. Where white Americans almost invariably saw a travesty of justice, the majority of black Americans seemed to see a *triumph* of justice—a vindication (finally!) of *la vraie morale.* Clearly, whatever inner voice is responsible for definitions of right and wrong had been saying very different things to different people.

———

Ours is a secular society. For the majority of educated citizens of the United States, God, though he may be present somewhere, no longer makes himself available to arbitrate legal or moral issues. (I do not accept the idea that God speaks through the voice of Pat Robertson or any other fundamentalist social critic.) In Haiti the situation is somewhat different; most Haitians have regular and personal contract with their gods, who speak to them directly on many pressing themes. (It must be admitted that the *loa* of Haitian vaudou have not done a very good job so far of sorting out the problems of social justice that remain as desperate in Haiti today as they ever were in the past.) I suspect that Haitians are more likely than we are to see some aspect of the divine when they look within themselves for moral guidance. Still, when we in the First World search ourselves for that wellspring of *la vraie morale,* we do seem to find something as apparently self-evident as if it had been set there by divine fiat. One's inner sense of justice appears to be so axiomatic that only extraordinary circumstances can move one to question whether it is absolutely true or whether it is shared by any or many others.[7]

At the crisis of Faulkner's novel *The Unvanquished,* the hero Bayard Sartoris has this thought: "At least this will be my chance to find out if I am what I think I am or if I just hope; if I am going to do what I have taught myself is right or if I am just going to wish I were."[8] Although *The Unvanquished* is a Civil War novel, the issue

---

7. For example, the aphorism that inspired this whole argument turns out to come not from Montesquieu at all, but from Pascal. In its entirety, it reads: *"La vraie éloquence se moque de l'éloquence, la vraie morale se moque de la morale, c'est à dire que la morale du jugement se moque de la morale de l'esprit—qui est sans règles." Les Pensées,* sec. I, at 4. Not only is the source quite different from what I supposed, but in the context of the complete sentence the phrase I expropriated might have a very different sense from my interpretation of it. And yet the whole fiasco seems to support the general point that our axiomatic principles may not be so securely founded as we assume they are.

8. William Faulkner, *The Unvanquished* (New York: Vintage, 1991), 215.

has nothing to do with race; rather it concerns the character's intention to replace one defining moral imperative, *Revenge all injuries,* with another, *Thou shalt not kill.* The shift from the first standard of moral value to the second should be familiar to anyone with a general knowledge of both the Old and New Testaments. But Sartoris's formulation of the problem as an implied question to himself has applications even broader than that. I believe that all people must ask themselves the same question, in some version, whenever they reach an important moral crossroads.

There is a huge operative difference between *what I have taught myself,* in Faulkner's text, and *what I know.* Expressed therein is perhaps the whole human potential for moral growth. But the education of one's sense of justice requires some sort of guidance, and on the rare occasions when we look closely we find that the moral guideposts are apt to be placed very differently for people of different races, nationalities, classes, historical periods, and so on. If that is true, then we live in conditions of complete moral relativism, although, for the most part, without knowing it.

BLANCHE McCRARY BOYD

WHO KILLED SUSAN SMITH?

During closing arguments in the guilt-or-innocence phase of the Susan Smith trial, the prosecutor's booming voice had filled the courtroom in Union, South Carolina. But in his final statement during the penalty phase, many of us sitting only midway back could barely hear him. Tommy Pope, the youngest solicitor ever elected in this state, was losing his crusade to have Susan Smith executed, and he seemed to know that. He glossed over the issue of motive, skipped the word evil, and stuck mainly with "the heinousness" of the crime. Pope, a tall, smooth-faced man with an engaging manner and an athlete's frame, raised his cadenced southern voice only once: "She may be sorry now, but was she sorry when she dropped that parking brake down?" Even in this moment of vehemence, Pope acknowledged Smith's remorse, which he had previously fought to disprove.

The day before, defense lawyer David Bruck had paraded a series of relatives and friends of Susan Smith into the witness box. Bruck, a slight, handsome man who holds his head forward like Woody Allen, is so quiet-spoken that the *New York Times* writer had complained in print.

The first to testify was Kay Dillard, who had taught math at Union High School for twenty-one years and had been Susan's teacher for three. Dillard's gray hair was pertly cut, her manner graciously no-nonsense. "Susan and I just became really good friends. She had such a warmth about her, she had a way of making people feel good about things." During her junior year, Susan confided to Dillard that her stepfather, Beverly Russell, was molesting her sexually. "[Susan] begged me not to go to the authorities" because she was concerned about her mother and about her family being ruined. Dillard said, "I didn't know what to do, but I listened." She called a psychologist friend to discuss Susan, then sent her to talk to a minister named Tom Currie. After Susan's graduation, she and her teacher stayed in touch. "Michael and Alex were her life. I thought Michael and Alex would be her salvation."

Bruck asked, "Do you have a basis for asking this jury for mercy for Susan Smith?"

Dillard turned her anguished, smiling face to the panel. "If Susan dies, I think that a part of me will die with her."

The trial of Susan Smith was deeply southern in its setting, its demeanor, and its participants, which is why Dillard smiled through her anguish and why she and those who followed her to the stand were so effective.

Bruck, a native of Canada, has lived and practiced in South Carolina for many years, but he will always be an outsider. Judy Clark, his co-counsel, is a tall Californian who wore tailored suits and no makeup; her dark blond hair was blunt cut with bangs that framed her intense blue eyes. This style of attractiveness was foreign in Union: During a break in the proceedings, I heard two southern women TV reporters discussing what a fine candidate Clark would be for their makeover show.

Because I grew up in Charleston, I am an insider and always will be, though I have lived and worked in the North for many years. My mother and the judge's mother play bridge and golf together, and my cousin Samm served on the executive committee of the state Republican Party with Beverly Russell. Samm's brother Glenn, a highly ranked Republican state senator, is a leader in the fight to keep the Confederate flag flying on top of the state house. Together Glenn and Samm own a gallery that specializes in Confederate art, where customers can also purchase reproductions of Confederate uniforms, tin cups, belt buckles, and "real" soap made of tallow, water, and caustic soda. There's a rack of bumper stickers that say things like "Don't Blame Us, We Voted for JEFF DAVIS"; my favorite features an image of a large, hungry mosquito saying "Send More Yankees, They Are Delicious!"

Union's courtroom was elegant and Faulknerian, with dark wood paneling and beautifully patterned high ceilings. It was large enough to accommodate the players, the families, fifty or sixty journalists, and at least seventy-five spectators daily. Because the judge had ruled that cameras could not record the proceedings, there were also twenty to twenty-five sketch artists sitting along the sides, in the front row, and in the gallery above. The scratching sounds of their pencils and pastels filled occasional silences.

Southerners are generally polite and unpretentious; perhaps it's too hot to be otherwise. Charleston traffic jams are characterized by an "Oh no, you go first" quality, and no driver is so ungracious as to blow a car horn. It was not surprising then to find the trial marked by very good manners. Judge William Howard was patient and respectful with potential jurors, and he offered tissues to witnesses who wept. The witnesses weren't polarized; sometimes folks called by the prosecution were called again by the defense. None of the lawyers showed any trace of argumentativeness, and the closest anyone came to personal attack was when the co-prosecutor remarked, "[S]omeone as smart as Mr. Bruck . . . " Bruck has lived in the South long enough to know he was being insulted.

Reasoning is distrusted in southern culture, which can lead outsiders to think we're stupid. The closest most southerners come to abstraction is balancing our checkbooks or betting on football games. We value narrative intelligence and understand best through stories, which is why Kay Dillard and Walt Garner and the other down-home folks who followed them were such powerful witnesses.

Walt Garner, white-haired at age fifty-one, has lived in Union all his life. His face is as gentle as Heidi's grandfather's. Garner works for a mill, his wife's name is Bobbie (Baub-a), and their daughter Donna is Susan's best friend. "We've known Susan real well since she started grammar school." Susan's children had stayed at his house a lot, and he was as close to them as any family member, especially to little Michael, who had been four. "He called me Walt. He followed me around." Michael believed he was helping Walt restore an old car in the garage: "He had his little tools, and I had mine." Michael's handprints are still on this car, and Walt has found himself unable to wash them off.

When the children were reported missing, Garner stayed up from Tuesday night till Thursday morning, driving around looking for them. In the nine days before Susan confessed, he didn't spend much time with his family "for the simple reason that I was out looking." The home of Linda and Beverly Russell, Susan's mother and stepfather, had become family headquarters, and Walt was there when "it came over the TV" that Susan had admitted drowning her children in John D. Long Lake. "Everybody was crying. . . . Everybody was real tore up, and some was actually sick." Walt's own reaction was disbelief. "I knew Susan loved those children too much. They were her life. In her right mind, she would never have hurt those kids."

When Bruck asked what the effect would be if Susan was executed, Walt Garner said, "I just don't know how our family could handle it. And we're not even immediate family."

Bruck then showed the jury a video clip of Walt Garner with the children. The sounds of Michael and Alex Smith's happy voices filled the courtroom. Susan began to rock forward and backward in her seat, looking rigidly straight ahead, but there was nothing she could do to prevent herself from hearing them.

Susan Smith looks ordinary, a pretty but conventional young woman, a good girl. In eight months of prison, she had gained weight, thickened, and her face had aged. The only sign of unruliness was her blond-streaked brown hair; some days she pulled it back into a pony tail, and other days it hung heavily down her back. The clothes she wore in court were plain, dowdy, mother-pleasing, church-going. She smiled occasionally, like someone who can't imagine what else to do.

After Walt Garner, a relative named Hedy Harrison took the stand. Hedy said fiercely, "I think Susan was a *wonderful* mother. I saw the love that Susan had for her children. They had a lot of love to give back, and I think that comes from being loved." The night before she confessed, Susan and Hedy had a brief moment alone at the house, and Susan said, "I wish I could turn back time." Hedy did not ask Susan what she meant, and, trying to explain why not, her face worked with emotion. "I just didn't want to listen to her hurting more than she was already hurting."

Next came Tomi Vaughan, who is married to William Vaughan, Susan's dead father's brother. Tomi is a registered nurse, and she was at the hospital when Susan was born. "I've known Susan since the minute she entered the world." Tomi described the impact of Susan's father's suicide. "It caused so much guilt. Seventeen years later, we're still asking ourselves, what could we have done?" Although Susan's mother remarried, Tomi saw Susan at family gatherings, weddings, and funerals. She noticed that Susan was very patient with her children, although she was "just a child herself." When Tomi found out what had happened to Michael and Alex Smith, she thought, "This can't have happened, Susan is not capable . . . we were devastated. I love Susan very much. I always will love Susan. We're just ordinary family. And we've had everything about our lives hung outside. But we love the Lord."

"Do you have a basis for asking this jury for mercy?"

"We cannot bear to lose her. We cannot bear the thought of Susan leaving us also."

To cross-examine these witnesses who spoke in the right accents, Tommy Pope alternated with his co-prosecutor, Keith Giese (pronouced Gee-say). Giese was not as tall as Pope, but he had that same well-scrubbed, engaging look, that easy way of moving. Both Giese and Pope have the aura of politicians-to-be, and this trial offered them many opportunities to get fitted for their futures. Although Bruck had managed to keep cameras out of the courtroom, Keith Giese had appeared on national television that very morning. Now his father was in the courtroom to watch his boy in action.

The senior Mr. Giese is a state senator, so, before court began, I introduced myself to him as Glenn McConnell's cousin. He shook my hand fervently and expressed his admiration for Glenn. When the senior Mr. Giese left during the midmorning break, he shrugged at me, smiled, and remarked that he just didn't get the point of this kind of testimony. Reasonably, I explained something Judge Howard had said earlier: The Smith case was unusual in that the family of the victims and the family of the perpetrator were the same. Therefore, victim impact testimony (that is, testimony of those who are suffering because of the victims' deaths) is relevant to the defense as well as to the prosecution. Many of those who loved Michael and Alex Smith love Susan Smith too. Mr. Giese shook his head and gave me a compassionate look, a look I remembered from high school when I would try to explain to my elders that, theoretically at least, Christianity and racial discrimination didn't mesh. This look said that someday, if I were lucky, I would get over my touching faith in reasoning.

The decision to try Susan Smith was extraordinary. She had already confessed to drowning her two children and, for more than six months, had offered to plead guilty and accept life imprisonment. (In South Carolina this would have made her eligible for parole in thirty calendar years; eligibility does not mean, of course, that a famous murderess would ever be freed.) The trial, then, was only formally important. The penalty phase—whether she would receive a death sentence—was its entire legal purpose.

Many people already thought that Tommy Pope's chance of getting a jury to vote for execution was small, especially in Smith's hometown. Sentiment in Union had been very much against her immediately after the confession, but in the ensuing months, angers had cooled, and deeper notions of Christianity, like forgiveness and leaving vengeance to God, became part of the common voice.

As solicitor, Pope had previously dealt with a murder case that had, apparently, similar motives. Richard Darnell Haynes, like Smith, had murdered his offspring, and from a similar motive: He wanted to die but hadn't been unable to kill himself. However, the murder of Haynes's child, who was four years old, was not an aborted suicide attempt: Haynes just smothered his son with a pillow and then turned himself in to police. Tommy Pope let Haynes plead guilty to manslaughter and sentenced him to six years in prison. When questioned about the difference in his treatment of these two cases, Pope denied that sexism was a factor. He argued that Smith's nine days of lying demonstrated a heartless, cynical character. He said that all he had to do was watch those video tapes of Susan pleading with that imaginary kidnapper to get fired up all over again.

———

The Smith trial had the grandeur and dramatic unity of a great play. Act I, which took place the first week, dealt with Susan's mental competence and with jury selection; it ended on a Saturday night with only two alternates chosen instead of the usual six because even Judge Howard (who was born in the North) seemed to understand the urgencies of narrative construction. Act II was the trial proper, which began on Monday and ended the following Saturday night with the jury finding Susan Smith guilty of two counts of murder. Act III was the penalty debate, which began on Monday and ended late afternoon on the following Friday with Smith sentenced to the term of imprisonment she had already offered to plead to.

Oscar Wilde asserted that life imitates art, and in the Smith trial narrative and fact converged in the form we now call creative nonfiction; this was high tragedy of peculiarly twentieth-century sort. Unlike the tales of Gary Gilmore and Jeffrey MacDonald, the protagonist here was a woman, and her classic flaw, according to the prosecutor, was lust; according to the defense, it was depression.

What made Gary Gilmore fascinating was his machismo, combined with his astounding literary eloquence. Gilmore challenged the state to kill him, yet he was able to articulate the conflicts that drove him with an exquisiteness that could be termed feminine. Gilmore provided Norman Mailer with the subject of what many think is his best book, *The Executioner's Song.* What made physician Jeffrey MacDonald such a large figure was the extreme contrast involved in the question of his guilt or innocence. Either he was a monster capable of killing his wife and two daughters with unthinkable violence who was then diabolical enough to surgically puncture his own lung to make himself appear a victim too, or else he was a victim too, a pitiable man who'd lost his family and was now being unjustly accused. There was no in-between possibility, and Joe McGinniss's book *Fatal Vision* brilliantly explored who the real monster was, MacDonald or the prosecution. (McGinniss now might think that the real monster is Janet Malcolm, but that is another story.)

Susan Smith first became psychically enormous because of her fervent lying. Her televised anguish and convincing appeals to a mythic black kidnapper to return her children unharmed thrust her into the public imagination as a victim. The story she embodied was extreme enough: the horrors of big-city violence and cruelty enter a small southern town where people don't look their doors. The perp was the bogeyman, another black male supposedly doing something unthinkable, carrying the public's imagination past carjackings with children thrown out of cars to a new level: the children actually taken, right into the void. The search for Michael and Alex Smith was immediate and large-scale, creating an ongoing daily real-life drama. As the days passed and neither the children nor the car turned up, suspicion grew that the void had been created by Susan Smith.

Nevertheless, her confession was stunning: The missing car was at the bottom of John D. Long Lake, and her children were strapped in their car seats inside it. Smith claimed that she had gone to the lake to commit suicide with her children and that the suicide attempt had gone awry. This account was not believed, partly because the pop situation required polarization: If Smith was not a victim, she must be a monster. The only missing element was motive, and when Susan's former boyfriend, Tom Findlay, released part of a letter he'd written to her in which he explained that one of the reasons he was breaking off their relationship was that he didn't want children, the evil image of Susan Smith achieved focus: Smith had murdered her children to try to hold onto her rich boyfriend.

Since Tom Findlay was the son of the owner of the town's major business, the Conso textile factory where Susan worked, and since Susan's estranged husband was a poor young man employed as an assistant manager at the Winn-Dixie, the issue of class now entered the picture. David Smith, Susan's husband, had been a sympathetic figure during the nine days the children were missing; he'd demonstrated absolute loyalty to Susan, and when the fate of his sons was known, his grief was awful to watch. The victims, then, were not only Susan's children, but her working-class hero of a husband. So the demonic depiction of Susan Smith developed shading, the illusion of depth.

Mothers who hurt or kill their children are, unfortunately, not that uncommon, and they tend to fall into two categories: those involved with substance abuse and those mired in depression. For the first group, tales of cruelty and callousness abound. But for the second group, there is rarely a history of poor mothering, and the murder of infants is chillingly mixed up with love. For suicidal mothers who are biologically and emotionally committed to protecting their offspring, the question of infanticide can be morally complex. If a mother thinks the world is such a bad place that she has no desire to live further in it, why would she leave her helpless children behind? In her confession, Smith wrote, "I felt I couldn't be a good mom anymore, but I didn't want my children to grow up without a mom. I felt I had to end our lives to protect us all from any grief or harm."

In her opening statement, Judy Clark said, "Suicide is why we are here. . . . The problem is the body's will to live, and Susan jumped out of that car. It's a whole lot easier to roll a car into the lake than to stay in it yourself." If the instinctive will to live pulled Smith out of the car, her religiosity may have been an underlying factor. Christians view suicide as a sin, and when she was a child, Smith had worried a great deal about whether her father had gone to heaven. She wrote, "My children are with our Heavenly Father now, and I know that they will never be hurt again." Her children might be safe with their heavenly father, but would Smith, dead by her own hand, have accompanied them?

The issue of suicide permeated all three weeks of the trial. The prosecution's psychiatrist, who evaluated Smith to see whether she was sane, took the stand during Act I, before jury selection was complete. Dr. Donald Morgan said that Smith was technically sane according to South Carolina standards, with one small complication: She should not testify. If she testified, she would not "self-protect". Although any defendant has the legal right to take the stand, Smith's right was impaired. "If she took the stand and described herself and described her feelings and told people that she was really guilty and deserved to die, I mean, I think that would be troubling, if I were her lawyer." Morgan did more for the defense than he did for the prosecution. He said that Smith was suicidal at present and had been suicidal the night the children drowned, and that she had been mentally ill that night and was mentally ill now with a major depression; he came close to having Smith declared incompetent. The only thing Dr. Donald Morgan did for the state's case (and this is a state in which suicide is a felony and the mentally ill may be executed) was show that the defendant met the narrow South Carolina definition of fitness for trial.

Like much great art, Smith's trial was shot through with irony. If she wished to die, why, then, was she cooperating with her lawyers' attempts to save her? And why did the state keep her under suicide watch for eight months to try to execute her? The state is not an institution that addresses its contradictions, but in a press conference David Bruck did try to account for Susan Smith's. Bruck said that Smith understood that her family had been through too much; if they had to endure her spending years on death row, they might not survive the strain.

Tommy Pope had bought the monstrous image of Susan Smith from the beginning and, through most of the trial, stubbornly clung to it. But on this last day of testimony in the penalty phase, as one after another of the friends and relatives of Susan Smith pleaded with the jurors, expressing their love and grief for her dead children, and their guilt and anguish over what they could have done, he began to seem uncertain. "Don't put another death on our consciences," these witnesses were saying, and "Don't ask us to go through the death of another person we love." Tommy Pope rose to cross-examine them, and his questions grew difficult to hear. He looked like a man understanding a theoretical point for the first time. He looked like a man realizing he might be wrong.

If the Smith trial had a weird beauty and release, these qualities arose directly from the ugly story it exposed. Despite its numinous air, the stage here was small; this was a community drama, intimate and claustrophobic. The sheriff was the godfather of Susan's brother's children, the police chief's wife was on the jury, and all jurors had followed the case. Figuratively, the whole town was in bed with each other. And literally, Susan Smith was in bed with too many of them. Southerners tend to be psychologically unselfconscious, to act out. Beverly Russell had been acting out with his stepdaughter since she was fifteen. He was not a sadistic abuser but one who seemed to confuse fondness with fondling. Like Jimmy Swaggart, Russell may have found the constrictions of Christianity irresistibly erotic. How else could he spend an evening hanging up Pat Robertson posters around Union and come home to enter his daughter's bedroom?

Testimony from a number of sources revealed Susan Smith to be a classic example of abuse. Tom Findlay said that Susan did not get sexual pleasure from physical intimacy, but merely liked the holding, the closeness. A defense psychiatrist said that Susan did not enjoy sex with Beverly Russell and often felt dreadful afterwards. Nevertheless, she had continued her relationship with Russell—perhaps even at her own initiation—right up until a few months before the children drowned. And she was promiscuous with others as well. The famous Tom Findlay breakup letter listed another obstacle to their relationship besides Susan's children. Findlay wrote about the necessity of being "a nice girl" and criticized Susan for having kissed and fondled a married man named Benjy Brown one night when a group of people were hanging out in Findlay's hot tub. The *Charlotte Observer* reported that Susan kissed Brown, put her hand on his leg, and said, "I know how to make you happy." Susan Smith's wish to receive love from men, especially older men, by giving them sexual pleasure may seem wretchedly sad to those of us who've been abused, but in the general culture her behavior was seen (and continues to be seen) as dangerous, whorish, immoral.

When David Smith first met Susan, they were both working at the Winn-Dixie. According to David, "Winn-Dixie is my own special world." In his as-told-to book *Beyond All Reason,* Smith described his attraction for the woman he would marry. "Susan had a million-dollar smile. She had pretty hair. She had a bigger chest than girls I had gone out with before." There were rumors about Susan and three other employees, two of whom were married men. "I didn't like hearing people laugh behind Susan's back. . . . Susan was a 'slut' or a 'whore,' dating a married man who was old enough to be her father, and sneaking around behind his back with someone else. I began to feel sorry for her. It degraded her, all the gossip." David explained how, after these relationships ended, Susan made a half-hearted suicide attempt, got hospitalized, and then took a month off from work. When she returned, David began dating her, although he was engaged to someone else. Susan got pregnant, and they decided to get married. Linda Russell insisted that her oft-fallen daughter wear off-white.

Not surprisingly, this marriage disintegrated quickly. Two days after their first anniversary, Susan, along with her son Michael, moved back to her parents' house. David began having an affair at work with a woman named Tiffany, and Susan began seeing Tom Findlay. The breakup of Susan and David was soapy and jealous, with scenes at the Winn-Dixie as well as the Conso Christmas party. David and Susan tried to reconcile, and it was while they were "dating"—a secret kept from Tiffany—that Susan got pregnant with Alex. David dumped Tiffany but soon (secretly, of course) began seeing her again. The night that Alex was born, David was supposed to meet Tiffany.

The divorce fight with David triggered Susan's suicide attempt and the deaths of their children. David, who had assumed they were going to dissolve their marriage amicably, had been very upset to be served papers that accused him of adultery. He didn't want his name or Tiffany's "dragged through the mud." Several days prior to the deaths of the children, David came over to the house, and he and Susan lay on the floor with Michael to help him fall asleep. Susan fell asleep too. David got up and went through her purse, where he found the letter from Tom Findlay. He was elated because it proved that Susan had been having an adulterous affair also. He took the letter with him to work at the Winn-Dixie, where Tiffany was just getting off her shift. There are no copy stores in Union, so Tiffany drove home, borrowed her mother's keys, and took the letter to the church where her mother was a secretary. In the dark, she used the church copier. She told David later, "It was spooky, being alone in the big dark church at midnight."

The next morning, David returned to Susan's and, while she was in the shower, put the original letter back into her purse. According to defense accounts, David was very nice to Susan this morning, taking the children to day care and cleaning the carpets; then he insisted on having sex. Afterwards he told Susan that he knew something that would change their divorce, but he wouldn't say what he knew.

Susan's affair with Tom Findlay was not much of a secret, but she did have two terrible secrets. David knew that her stepfather had molested her while she was in high school, but he did not know that the relationship had continued. Nor did he know this: some six months before, Susan had had an affair with her boss, Carey Findlay, who was Tom's father. Susan feared that David Smith had tapped her phone and learned this. If so, Susan would lose not only Tom Findlay, she would lose her job, and her family would be disgraced. The day the children died, she told Tom Findlay about her relationship with his father, presumably to reach him before David did. Tom reacted very coldly. Later that afternoon, she went to Tom's office and said she didn't know why she'd made up that crazy stuff about his father, and here was his Auburn sweatshirt back. Tom, sensing her suicidal frame of mind, responded with surprising tenderness. No, Susan, he wanted her to wash the sweatshirt and give it back to him later. He told her he would always be her friend. Later that night, about eight o'clock, when Tom was at the local hangout called Hickory Nuts, he asked a couple of friends, Benjy

Brown among them, to step outside with him. He was worried, he told them, that Susan Smith might hurt herself.

When David Smith first learned that his children were missing, he couldn't understand how that had happened. After all, he'd had Tiffany following Susan all day. When Susan left Tom Findlay at his office, she'd driven home with her children. Tiffany, who watched her pull into her driveway, assumed that Susan was home for the night. Tiffany checked again around 7:30 P.M., but Susan's car was gone.

Susan had called her mother and asked if she could come over with Michael and Alex. Her mother explained that she was going to watch her other grandchildren play football and wouldn't be home till nine. So Susan Smith drove around for awhile. "I felt like things could never get any worse." If she ended her life, her affair with Carey Findlay would not be exposed, and she would not hurt Tom or her family. "As I rode and rode and rode, I felt even more anxiety coming upon me about not wanting to live." She ended up at John D. Long Lake with time to kill.

Beverly Russell had been absent throughout the trial, but on one particular day, after lunch, he was sitting in the front row just behind Susan. There was tension about whether he would testify, but Chekhov said if you hang a gun on the wall in Act I you must fire it by Act III. Like Susan Smith, Beverly Russell looked ordinary. Dressed neatly in a dark suit, he was a big, mournful man with the sad eyes of a basset hound.

The first defense witness after lunch turned out to be a guard from the Women's Correctional Center in Columbia, where Susan Smith had spent the last eight months in isolation under suicide watch. At 8 A.M. that morning, Felicia Mungo had been unexpectedly subpoenaed, so she was still wearing her uniform. A black woman who'd been working for Corrections for two years, Mungo was assigned to Susan's tier and her cell; Mungo was responsible for checking on Susan every ten or fifteen minutes and for watching her on a twenty-four-hour video surveillance. Mungo described her charge's narrow cell, its spare furnishings, and her emotional state. "Sad, depressed, always worried about her mother . . . very sorry, talks about her boys, about suicide, wonders if they're gonna forgive her." Did Susan show any sign of racial prejudice? No, and she would apologize for saying a black man did it. She doesn't treat black and white different. She was not manipulative at all. She was cooperative. "Doesn't bother us. Just if she wants somebody to talk to."

"She wants somebody to talk to?"

"All the time. When she doesn't know we're looking at her, she's on her knees, crying reading her Bible. . . . She tries to hide it, how sad she is . . . she knows she's to blame. She puts the blame on no one else."

Next the defense called Reverend Tom Currie to the stand. Currie, the minister Kay Dillard had sent Susan to see when she was still in high school, had such a powerful voice he didn't need a microphone. Currie said he'd had a second meeting with Susan about a year ago, when she'd been separated from David Smith and was trying to decide whether to get a divorce. Currie had not seen her since her arrest.

As a minister, Currie had counseled two other women who were survivors of sexual abuse. He'd saved the life of one of these women: "I took her off a closet door where she was hanging." As a community leader, he'd been part of a group of fifteen ministers who'd gathered at the courthouse pleading for the return of the children. After Susan confessed, he explained how the community had been traumatized. There was a sense of betrayal, of hurt, a great deal of anger. Many people couldn't get the image of the children out of their minds. In his resonant voice, Currie said his job was "to remind people of their spiritual resources." He said that when Tommy Pope was evaluating whether to seek the death penalty, he had asked for community response. Currie wrote two personal letters, but he didn't get a reply. "This community needs a closure, needs to bring this to an end. If Susan gets the death penalty, this will drag on."

"Do you have a basis for asking this jury for mercy?"

Currie faced them and said with great force, "For me, life in prison satisfies justice. The death penalty would be more vengeance than justice."

When Pope rose to cross-examine this witness, he made the mistake of saying something to the effect of "You wouldn't be preaching to this jury, would you?"

"I certainly am," Currie replied. By the time Reverend Tom Currie was finished, Pope looked almost shamefaced, like a very young man who had been dragged by the ear to the principal's office.

The defense called Beverly Russell, and he took the stand. "She's my stepdaughter," he said gently, and smiled at her.

Bruck focused first on the nine days of Susan's deception. Russell described how she'd been staying "at my . . . our house." He got rid of the handguns, just as he had once before, when she was depressed at the age of thirteen. Since Russell was politically experienced, he knew how to get media attention. "I went into a campaign mode, to find those boys."

Russell's face became increasingly drawn, sad, and the first time he mentioned Michael and Alex by name, he began to cry. He told how his house had been full of people, so he'd moved the children's toys into his stepson's room. There was a wading pool with Michael's and Alex's toys in it. When he returned to the house around 8 A.M. the next morning, he heard "an extreme, wailing cry. I thought we must have gotten some news. . . . Susan was layin' on the floor wailing, holding one arm in the pool with the toys." Russell called a doctor, who prescribed a sedative. Sedation continued for the entire nine days.

Bruck showed a video of Russell with Michael and Alex, and Russell kept wiping his eyes. Yes, he and Linda spent a lot of time with the boys. Yes, regular Sunday dinner, and they didn't go home till dark. "Were you close to those boys?" "Oh, yes." He talked about the problem of how to explain the situation to his other grandchildren. He talked about his wife's difficulty in accepting what had happened. He said, his voice rising, "We can't get to the grieving process for Michael and Alex, we're so focused on trying to save Susan."

Time for the most difficult subject, incest. Once again Bruck found the high road. He asked Beverly Russell to read a letter he'd written to Susan on Father's Day. Russell read, weeping: "I must tell you how sorry I am in letting you down as a father. . . . If I had known at the time what the result of my sin would be, I would have found the strength to behave according to my responsibilities. I was the most important male figure in your life. When I came into the family, you leaned on me and looked to me for support and love, but when the line was crossed I failed you, Linda, God, and the rest of my family. . . . And all you needed from me was the right kind of love."

His words had the simplicity of grief. Like many of the witnesses in this trial, Beverly Russell's suffering seemed to burn away everything false, and he came across not as a monstrous figure, but as a pitiful one.

In his cross-examination, Tommy Pope brought out the fact that Susan had continued her sexual relationship with Russell after she reached the age of consent, but he was unable to make Susan sound lustful or evil; Russell's self-blame was simply too strong.

At the end of the day, with the jury out of the room, Judge Howard questioned Susan about her right to testify and her right to remain silent. Susan was wearing a black crepe blouse, and her hair was pulled back. She stood up beside her slight, handsome lawyer, who said, "She is not going to testify. It's her decision, but she has relied on our advice."

"Ms. Smith, please, ma'am. You have a right to testify. Is it *you* who is making this decision?" the judge asked several times. "Yes sir," she said quietly. "Yes sir."

The jury was called back in. The defense rested. Tommy Pope said the state would offer no rebuttal.

There would be other moving, fascinating moments in the trial of Susan Smith: the judge's charge to the jury would be the result of brilliant lawyering by Bruck, and his closing argument would be both wonderful writing and effective theater; the jurors would

deliberate only two and a half hours before unanimously rejecting
the death penalty (they did not have to be unanimous), and several
reportedly asked the judge if Susan Smith would receive, in prison,
the psychological help she needs. But this day, when the chorus of
friends and relatives chanted their love and guilt and Beverly Russell came onto the stage and fell upon his sword, this day provided
a classical catharsis for Susan Smith, her family, and her community.
On this day Susan Smith was sentenced to life.

The law, like other forms of storytelling, imposes structure on
the chaos of experience, assigning meaning and responsibility. The
Smith trial revealed that people who love each other and try to do
their best can end up with lies, deceit, suicide, incest, and even a
double murder. Susan Smith was responsible for the deaths of
Michael and Alex Smith because, no matter what her mental state
might have been, she could not, as Tommy Pope pointed out, "suicide another person." Smith may have seen her children as an extension of herself, but they were legal people nevertheless. And
Beverly Russell may have had ego and boundary problems, but
statutory rape and incest are moral crimes.

The verdict for Beverly Russell and others is personal: to wade
forever in the dark waters of guilt and regret. The clumsy machina-
tions of the law decreed that Susan Smith will spend her life in
prison. When her sentence was announced, the gods concurred: In
the hot, dusty town of Union, a drenching rain washed down.

JOHN CASEY

JUSTICE AS A NOURISHER OF NARRATIVE

Sometimes justice is easy: There's just the two of us. You and I have our eye on the piece of cake. I say, "You cut, I choose."

How readily comprehensible that system is, how perfectly *symmetrical,* how self-contained, how portable through space and time wherever there are conflicting desires, communication, and reason.

Perhaps you would prefer to flip a coin? That's fair, in the sense of equal opportunity, but the symmetry lasts only as long as the coin is in the air. It takes a wonderfully metaphysical loser to be satisfied with savoring the vanished chance while the winner has had her equal opportunity and is eating it too.

There are more instances and more theories than I would dare to explore, even when dealing with divvying up desserts. What I'd like to get to however, is this: Whatever instances or theories of justice we're working with, there is—even before an invocation of a rule or rules—an imaginative process. And this imaginative process is one that has a great deal in common with the imaginative process that is useful in making up a good story. It requires an adversarial imagination. To be a good adversary, you have to figure out what you want and what the other person wants. Wanting, needing, and claiming for yourself require somewhat less imagination.

When I first started teaching fiction writing at the University of Virginia, I happened to get a spate of love stories from my students, forlorn and aggrieved love stories. If the writer was a *he,* the story was she-done-him-wrong. If the writer was a *she,* it was the other way around. These stories had something else in common: They were far too long.

As much by way of self-defense as by way of considered aesthetics, I started asking him to rewrite his story from her point of view, and her from his. All the rewritten stories were much shorter and much more interesting. Several of them even became good.

"Stresses and strains," my old high school English teacher used to say. "It's all stresses and strains." By which he meant writing is construction, is engineering, and that buildings and compositions stay upright by pushes and equaling pulls.

Was it push equaling pull that made these stories better? The push of the lyric self-lament (sometimes in the original draft thinly veiled in the third person, sometimes full-frontal first person) was still the initiating force of the story, but in the revised version the push was checked hard by the pull of the other point of view, so that the rewritten story, although *assigned* to be *entirely* from the other point of view, came out balanced. The strategies the students applied were various. Some wrote he-said-she-said versions. Some *did* write from the other point of view but managed to undermine, at least partially, the laments and justifications of the other.

I filed this away in my mind as a version of the FCC equal-time doctrine. I thought this was a clearer and easier slogan than my English teacher's somewhat gnomic "stresses and strains." I now think I may have been careless. The equal-time doctrine accounts for the increased fairness, in the verse balance, in the students' stories, but not for the stories becoming shorter and better. I now think that stresses and strains—some sort of conflict, competition, ordeal, or at least adversary proceeding—are helpful elements in the art of fiction.

Another English teacher of mine, in a lecture on Joyce's *Portrait of the Artist as a Young Man,* pointed out that *Portrait of the Artist* is organized into three parts: lyric, dramatic, and epic. In the lyric stage the protagonist is trying to determine his identity and the boundaries of his identity: what is him and what is not him. The point of view is single. At first it is swaddled in a cocoon. Even when encountering the world, the self is the subject and everything else is other. Everything else is an object of desire or a hostile force or a backdrop to the emergence and growth of the self. For the dramatic stage of literature to come into being, a lyric self must recognize that there is at least one other self populating this universe of everything else, another self capable of similar desires, feelings, and communication. The desires of the other may conflict with those of the protagonist or at least overlap, and the story is now concerned with that conflict as much as with the development of self. The dramatic is not necessarily a higher or better stage. The lyric can be intense, deep, and coherent, as in Proust. Marcel—the primary self if you put aside the interstitial story of Swann—sends out his senses like a swarm of bees, and they gather so much of France, of nature, and of civilization that in the end Marcel has filled his hive with overflowing combs of honey.

Nor is the epic, which won't detain us long, necessarily a higher or better stage. A short definition of an epic is a story in which the fate of the protagonist is coterminous with the fate of his or her tribe or nation: Aeneas leads the defeated Trojans on a voyage and ends up starting Rome. The end of the *Portrait of the Artist as a Young Man* is mock epic: "I go now to forge the conscience of my race in the unfettered society of my soul." (I confess that when I first read that sentence as a young man I was especially thrilled. I didn't get the mock part. The title of the work is quite rightly *Portrait of the Artist as a Young Man.*

But you don't necessarily get to choose, and often the dramatic story is thrust upon you. So back to the dramatic. In law school I took a seminar called "Theories of Justice." One of the early notions was that a person can't have a concept of justice until she or he recognizes that there are other beings endowed with a capacity for feeling, desire, communication, and reason. This preliminary condition is the same as that necessary for dramatic literature, with the addition of reason.

Aristotle says, "Among friends, there is no justice." By which he means that if you love your friend, you wish for her all good things, whereas justice is concerned with dividing up good things when two or more people want them and good things are in short supply.

About halfway into *Splendeurs et Misères des Courtisanes,* Balzac, writing at his usual headlong pace, found that two of his main characters, a man and a woman, had fallen in love and were living happily in a cozy house in an ideal setting. So he wrote this remarkable sentence: "The history of happiness is boring, so we shall skip the next five years." And with a stroke of his pen, he flung the pair of them back into the perilous currents of Parisian intrigue.

Suppose Aristotle and Balzac are right. Do we hunger after conflict in our reading as much as we hunger after justice in life?

There are some people—and some parts of most of us—that do hunger after a story with sharp edges, in literature and in life. This hunger can take unpleasant forms—for instance, voyeurism or schadenfreude. We even sometimes watch trials as a mob. One of the justifications for criminal trials is that we have to do something by way of retribution or we would act as a mob. Better a judicial process that gives the people their day in court. So we may watch a trial hoping to see a villain punished, both by the spectacle and by the sentence. And there is a literature that panders to this: *Death Wish* starring Charles Bronson, superhero stories, and patriotic war films. But there is a more important way that we take in both trials and stories. A story that troubled me in Sunday school was the one about King Solomon and the two women, each of whom claimed a baby. King Solomon heard their arguments, both of which were plausible. King Solomon's advisers were no help. King Solomon then said, "Since we can't decide, we'll divide the baby between you—by cutting it in half." The one true mother shrieked and told Solomon to give the baby to the other woman. The troublesome part comes from sympathy for the mother who believes Solomon. For an instant he uses his royal and judicial power to put her on the rack. And then he makes it all right.

So he's okay. But it isn't his story that interests me. The question that interests me is this: Is the mother worse off by reason of pain and suffering than before she got into this story? Or is she just the same in the end, the law having "made her whole"? Or is she better off?

One aftermath of the story I imagine goes something like this: Her screaming "No!" and then saying that the other woman should take her child opened her up to a larger love for her child. And perhaps she felt herself larger and stronger and proud of her instincts—fulfilled as much by them as by the decision of the court.

The point I'm after here is that the vise of the dramatic contest, of the judicial proceeding, brought the mother to a perfected state of herself and to a perfected utterance.

I find myself shocked by this reasoned praise of agony. Is it too mandarin? Or only too mandarin a way of speaking of an event if it were real life? Is it okay if I'm just taking a connoisseur's approach to a made-up story?

I'm trying to draw on my notions of law and adversary proceedings and use them to learn something about what purpose they serve in fiction. But, as often happened in law school, I tend to linger over the possibilities of the case as story rather than the story as case.

The next question: Is contest by itself a good thing? When you start out writing either scripts or stories and you ask an old hand to read them, one of the things that almost always gets said is "But where's the conflict?" And I've been suggesting here that that's a good thing to ask. But there's more to it than that. As I stated earlier, the precondition of a notion of justice is that at least two beings in the world recognize each other as having similar capacities for feeling, desire, communication, and reason.

Another way of saying that someone has a capacity for reason is to say that someone is sane. In our legal system we don't enforce contracts with insane people; we don't punish them for crimes if they don't know what they're doing and can't tell right from wrong. In some ways this is merciful. In some ways it is harsh—by excluding someone from justice we exclude her from humanity. There can still be a struggle, but it's only for control in the sense of dealing with a stray dog. Not quite—we don't kill insane people if they're unclaimed or unadopted after a week at the SPCA. Which, by the way, was what the Nazis did. They cut off food deliveries to insane asylums, a policy consonant with their more general theory of who was human and who subhuman. But we do deprive insane people of most general legal intercourse, both its responsibilities and possibilities.

And, in a similar manner, we don't generally find them useful as adversaries in stories. (There is an important exception: There is an adversary proceeding in our legal system to determine insanity, and there are good stories—sometimes lyric, sometimes dramatic—of a person's efforts either to regain sanity or to enlarge our notion of who is insane.)

I used to decree to my writing students that they shouldn't use drugs, drink, dreams, or delirium as a way of opening up a character in a story. The good students could always point to good stories that use one of the four devices. The good writers could write good stories that did. But in general I think there is both a loss of compression and a loss of focus in dramatic stories when one of the main characters loses a capacity to recognize the other as similar, and I think that loss is a component of delirium. And what interests me both about justice and drama is not just the recognition of similarity but also that the adversary proceedings usually result in some acknowledgment. Some aspects of our own characters are hidden, either from others, or from ourselves, or both. We are often insufficient in ourselves to find our full measure of vice or virtue, or, something that is perhaps more important, what Richard Rorty calls our "final vocabulary." He means by that not just a person's terminology but a person's sense of things, notions of what values one values most.

Why couldn't perilous adventure serve the same purpose? The hero pitted against the sea, a mountain, a monster. To some extent it does. There are stresses and strains. There is a contest. But what is lacking is the reflective quality, the sense that one adversary is a mirror of the other, even if distorted.

One way to illustrate this point is to consider ghost stories. Most ghost stories have a simple plot. It's "Boo!" The ghost is a disaster force like a tornado. One exception to this is a Henry James story called "The Jolly Corner." It starts in an almost infuriatingly leisurely and finicky way. The hero had left New York years before. Resisting family pressure to become a businessman, he went to Europe and tried to become civilized. He now finds New York more hectic, coarse, and combative than when he left. He has returned because he has inherited a house that he always loved. But soon enough we realize that the house is haunted. It is haunted by a more interesting ghost than the usual chain-clanking specter. It is haunted by himself, by the self he would have become had he not gone off to Europe. It is himself endowed with power and shrewdness, but devoid of sensibility and cultured intimacy. The hero has to acknowledge that this monster is part of him, that he is not simply a creature of his sojourn in civilized Europe, that there are energies in himself that are fierce and even dangerous, and that he will have to bend them into his life.

One of the most helpful criticisms I've received came from my eldest daughter, herself a writer. She read a rough draft of the eight hundred or so pages of a novel I've been working on. It is in part about family life. She seemed to accept the representations of conflict as fair and the three points of view as carrying more or less equal weight. All the main characters take their lumps, both from events and from critiques by the other characters. There was equal time; there were symmetrical stresses and strains. Yet she thought something was missing from the main male character.

She said, "He doesn't acknowledge . . . "

I said, "Acknowledge what?"

She said, "Acknowledge enough."

That was just right at the time. Another question that I have is whether acknowledgment is part of the outcome of justice/drama or part of the process. I'm now thinking of acknowledgment as owning up. To answer this question we have to consider whether we think that pressure can make people tell the truth. I think not. But I think a person under pressure, with no possibility of evasion, can be made to show something that gives a clue. When Solomon put pressure on the mother, she uttered what amounts to a lie, but her verbal act and her demeanor allowed Solomon to guess the truth.

I was once called as a witness at a child custody hearing. Testifying at a trial can be a frustrating, frightening, and brutal experience. It is not just taking an oath administered by the state or standing up to speak in the face of members of your community. There is, under cross-examination, a severe restriction on how much you can say, how much you can explain. The sensation is very like being strapped down on an operating table and being dissected, and the dissector is not someone who is operating for your benefit. What you've said on direct examination is repeated back to you in rearranged and truncated phrasing, sometimes repeated back to you in a tone of sneering disbelief. You tend to forget that the opposing slate of witnesses are going to go through the same thing. You tend to forget that there is any help available from the lawyer who called you or from the judge. You certainly don't think that this cross-examiner, this officer of the court, is playing fair with your honest testimony.

Afterwards, you feel humiliated. You feel you've been revealed as nervous, awkward, unconvincing, blundering, irresolute, confused, and weak. You wish you'd been bolder, stronger, louder—a regular Patrick Henry. And you haven't even been on trial; you've only been a witness.

What's the point? What has this degrading adversarial experience to do with truth or justice? The hopeful answer is this: that you have been pressed hard, and all your awkwardness, quavering, and faltering will be understood as the demeanor of a normal person under stress. Perhaps more—perhaps the finder of fact, whether judge or jury, will be able to read more from your unveiled demeanor than you could have conveyed in words alone. It is conventional wisdom that lawyers make lousy witnesses. They foresee the maneuverings of the cross-examiner and can step back and cover themselves. They can come out without a scratch. And nothing comes of it, except perhaps a suspicion that something has been concealed.

All this may be optimistic as regards the operation of justice in our legal system. There are lots of ways in which the process can go wrong. Among other things, it depends on alert, disinterested, and humanely intuitive finders of fact (the sort of people a writer would like as readers). And that takes us back to the comparison of the practice of justice and the practice of story writing.

I'm not saying that you need a formal setting for the cross-examination of your fictional characters, or even that the cross-examination be included in the final presentation of the story—just that anytime a character is rolling along unchecked by any other character's wishes, either the writer as director or the writer in the role of another character should set up an impediment that may correct for one side getting to be the only ones we recognize and care for as similar to ourselves.

Shakespeare is full of such moments. The plainest ones occur when a despised character turns on one or more of the privileged characters. An example of this occurs in *The Merchant of Venice*. Shylock is the villain of the comedy. When proposing the terms of his loan—the famous pound of flesh as guarantee—he pretends it's just a joke. He's as much as saying that there's no forfeiture at all because what good is a pound of Antonio's flesh? But near the end, when he has the chance to enforce it, he is the utter villain of the melodramatic portion of the play. Portia, in her capacity as judge, appears to decide in Shylock's favor.

PORTIA: [to Antonio] Therefore lay bare your bosom.

SHYLOCK: Ay, 'his breast': So says the bond: doth it not, noble judge?—'Nearest his heart': those are the very words.

PORTIA: It is so. Are there balance here to weigh the flesh?

SHYLOCK: I have them ready.

PORTIA: Have by some surgeon, Shylock, on your charge to stop his wounds, lest he do bleed to death.

SHYLOCK: Is it so nominated in the bond?

PORTIA: It is not so expressed, but what of that? 'Twere good you do so much for charity.

SHYLOCK: I cannot find it: 'tis not in the bond.

So at the beginning of the play Shylock is guileful, and near the end so devoid of humanity that his sensibility is shriveled and brittled to the size and stiffness of a clause in his contract.

Only in the middle of the play do we sense him as human, and that in his answer to a question from a gentleman of Venice who asks "if he forfeit, thou wilt not take his flesh: What's that good for?"

SHYLOCK: To bait fish withal: if it feed nothing else, it
            will feed my revenge. He hath disgraced me,
            and hindered me half a million, laughed at my
            losses, mocked at my gains, scorned my na-
            tion, thwarted my bargains, cooled my
            friends, heated mine enemies; and what's his
            reason? I am a Jew. Hath not a Jew eyes? Hath
            not a Jew hands, organs, dimensions, senses,
            affections, passions? Fed with the same food,
            hurt with the same weapons, subject to the
            same diseases, healed by the same means,
            warmed and cooled by the same winter and
            summer as a Christian is? If you prick us, do
            we not bleed? If you tickle us, do we not
            laugh? If you poison us, do we not die? And if
            you wrongs us, shall we not revenge? If we are
            like you in the rest, we will resemble you in
            that. If a Jew wrong a Christian, what is his
            humility? Revenge. If a Christian wrong a
            Jew, what should his sufferance be by Christ-
            ian example? Why, revenge. The villainy you
            teach me I will execute, and it shall go hard
            but I will better the instruction.

The general modern readership and audience tend to remember this famous speech as a plea for tolerance—"If you prick us, do we not bleed?" But it is more angry and defiant than that. Shylock lists the ways in which Antonio has wronged him, and when he says, "I am just like you," he isn't saying "I am just like you, so be nicer to me." He's saying "I'm just like you, and what would you do? You've taught me by your example. Revenge." It's not a speech that asks for recognition of the similarity of *virtues* between the Venetian Christians and Jews: it's more like Baudelaire's demand for recognition: *hypocrite lecteur, mon semblable, mon frère. Mirror* acknowledgment for good or ill.

I wish Shakespeare had written Shylock as more of an antagonist and less a villain, but you can't have everything. *The Merchant of Venice* is a comedy, and in comedy the characters, classically, are worse than we are. The point is that Shylock is given his moment of defiance, and it is his defiance that stands the play upright and makes us glimpse a similar soul, rather than an automaton running on the fuel of a single humor. This was a world in which the kings of several European countries, including England, had alternately borrowed money from their Jewish subjects and expelled them.

It was also an old world that was beginning to colonize the new. There was some question among the Europeans about whether the inhabitants of this brave new world had souls—which is to say, were they human?

In *The Tempest* there is a scene early on in which Prospero summons Caliban.

> PROSPERO: Thou poisonous slave, got by the divel himself upon thy wicked dam, come forth.

They put a few curses on each other, and then Caliban reminds Prospero (and us) of their original relationship.

> CALIBAN: This island's mine by Sycorax my mother,
> which thou takest from me! When thou camest first
> Thou strok'st me, and made much of me;
> would'st give me
> Water with berries in't, and teach me how
> To name the bigger light and how the less,
> That burn by day and night; and then I lov'd thee
> And show'd thee all the qualities o'th' isle,
> The fresh springs, brine pits, barren places and fertile.

Curs'd be I that did so! All the charms
Of Sycorax—toads, beetles, bats—light on
you!
For I am all the subjects that you have,
Which first was mine own king, and here
you sty me
In this hard rock, whiles you do keep from me
The rest o'th' island.

It's a good brief for an enslaved Adam. In the next exchange, however, Caliban is named villain and confesses to it.

PROSPERO: Thou most lying slave,
             Whom stripes may move, not kindness! I
             have us'd thee—
             Filth as thou art—with human care and
             lodg'd thee
             In mine own cell, till thou dids't seek to violate
             The honor of my child.
CALIBAN: Oho! Oho! Would't had been done!
             Thou dids't prevent me; I had peopl'd else
             This isle with Calibans.
MIRANDA: Abhorred slave,
             Which any print of goodness wilt not take,
             Being capable of all ill: I pitied thee,
             Took pains to make thee speak, taught thee
             each hour
             One thing or other; when thou didst not,
             savage,
             Know thine own meaning, but wouldst
             gabble like
             A thing most brutish, I endow'd thy
             purposes
             With words that made them known, but thy
             vild race—
             Though thou didst learn—had that in't
             which good natures

Could not abide to be with; therefore wast
thou
Deservedly confin'd into this rock,
Who hadst deserv'd more than a prison.

CALIBAN: You taught me language and my profit on't
Is, I know how to curse.

After this brave defiance—"I had peopled else/This isle with
Calibans" and "You taught me language and my profit on't/Is, I
know how to curse"—Caliban is shuffled off into the comic relief
with Trinculo and Stephano, a couple of sots whom he mistakes for
his saviours. In the very end Caliban gets to be part of the general
amnesty Prospero declares.

PROSPERO: Go, sirrah, to my cell;
Take with you your companions—as you look
To have my pardon, trim it handsomely.

CALIBAN: Ay, that I will and I'll be wise hereafter
And seek for grace! What a thrice double-ass
Was I to take this drunkard for a god
And worship this dull fool.

I wonder what happens after Prospero leaves the island, having
given up his magic powers and regained his title to Milan. Does
Caliban get his island back? You could stage it so that it appears
so—Caliban romping about the rocks as the Europeans stand on the
shore waiting for their ships to take them back to their cities and
the wedding between Miranda and Ferdinand.

That would be a happy end, a resolution as cozy as Job getting a
new herd of sheep, camels, oxen, and she asses. I've always thought
that restitution to Job was somewhat ornamental and anticlimactic.
Job's vindication and reward is that, having declared who he is and
what his claims are, the Lord answers him. This was the very thing
that Job's comforters told him was impossible. The comforters say
that Job must have broken one of the clauses of the covenant, it
should be just a clerical matter of rereading the rules. They say you
can't address the Lord. But Job insists on himself, on his knowledge

of himself. He declares who he is and who he conceives the Lord to be, not in detail, but in mysterious living essence. The Lord appears and, having declared who he is—the creator of all things—says to Job's comforters "Ye have not spoken of me the thing that is right as my servant Job hath."

If you think of justice as a set of rules, the way the comforters do, the Book of Job is perplexingly unfair. The initial setup is that Satan gets to torture Job on a dare. *Part* of the reason for the perplexity is that the Book of Job is an assemblage of different writings, by different authors, probably at different times. But the genius of it, in the parts sandwiched between the old-folktale beginning and the folktale ending, is Job's standing on his definition of himself. He is a creature of the Lord to be sure—"Hast thou not poured me out as milk, and curdled me like cheese?," but a creature with an identity and a knowledge of that identity, who therefore can ask the identity of his antagonist. The answer is overwhelming. Whoever wrote the Lord's recitation of the order of things—the part where God speaks to Job out of the whirlwind—was as brilliant as the writer of Genesis, of which this nature poem is a recapitulation in equally magnificent but less benign terms. This revelation, this acknowledgment of identity, of Job's standing, and of Job's having said the right thing are the award and fulfillment of Job's trial.

Jung wrote an essay on Job, a blend of humanist psychology and belief. The main point of it is that Job's function as a creature of God is to remind God that he is not only all powerful, but to recall him to his goodness.

The only villain in Job, by the way, is Satan. The three comforters (there is a fourth but he comes in late and to my mind doesn't add a lot) are good. They are earnestly trying to help. This is what they do when they first come to him. "So they sat down with him upon the ground seven days and seven nights, and none spoke a word unto him: for they saw that his grief was very great."

Another notion that has been creeping up on me is that I have a fondness for stories in which the characters oppose each other not out of ill will but out of blind or partly occluded good intentions.

To some extend I'm qualifying Aristotle's remark, "Among friends there is no justice." He's speaking of distributive justice, the pie-sharing. A silly and sweet example of blind good intentions is O. Henry's "The Gift of the Magi." A more elaborate case is Joyce Cary's trilogy *Herself Surprised, The Horse's Mouth,* and *To Be a Pilgrim.* Each volume is narrated by its protagonist, and while you are reading each one you are sympathetic to the wishes of each of the three characters. They cause each other a great deal of grief over the years through their pursuing the wishes that are consonant with their natures, but none is anything like a villain. The writer is just—in the simple sense of equal time, in the sense of symmetry (equal weight, equal sympathy on the part of the writer and reader), and in the most important sense of having the characters both oppose each other and sense each other as similar beings, maddening to each other because they must acknowledge each other and fulfilling to each other because each acknowledgment of another is an increase in one's own dimensions.

The examples of storytelling I've mentioned—from my sophomores' love stories up through O. Henry, Henry James, Joyce Cary, Shakespeare's *The Merchant of Venice* and *The Tempest,* and the Book of Job—have always struck me as having something to do with my notion of justice. At first I did think it was as simple as an equal-time doctrine. Then I reverted to the stresses-and-strains theory: something like a Newton's third-law conception of conflict—"For every action there is an equal and opposite reaction," and that it was the writer's job to create that symmetry. I'm not throwing these constructs aside as useless. But I have begun to think that a more crucial element of justice—the one most important to storytellers deploying their fictitious people—is found at that passage from lyric to dramatic, that first shiver of yourself in your own skin when you realize simultaneously that you can make claims, and that there is someone else who can make claims on you. That acknowledgment of another being is a preliminary, and when all is said and done, it is also the *outcome*—more than camels and she asses, more than a fair share of the island—that we would value most—that our adversary see and acknowledge our likeness one to the other.

MICHAEL DORRIS

THE MYTH OF JUSTICE

Where did we ever get the idea that life is ultimately fair? Who promised that there was a balance to things, a yin and yang that perfectly cancels each other out, a divine score sheet that makes sure that all the totals eventually ring even? Who exactly reaps what they sow? Does everything that goes around come around?

If that's some people's experience, I haven't met them, and my guess is, if they still believe it, they simply haven't lived long enough to know better.

Justice is one of those palliative myths—like afterlife with acquired personality and memory intact—that makes existence bearable. As long as we can think that our experience of being periodically screwed by fate is the exception to the rule we can hope for, as they used to say in commercials, a brighter tomorrow. As long as we can trust in an ultimate squaring of accounts, we can suffer what we assume to be temporary setbacks, transitory stumbles on our path toward redemption through good works and sacrifice.

When I was a child we were told of a Golden Ledger in which God (or one of his executive assistants) kept tabs on our every plus and minus, and as long as we wound up in the black we were "in"— as *in* heaven for all eternity. Our journey through the years as a test that was passable, if only we stretched hard enough. We were in control of our destinies. We were, at worst, Job: Hang in there, and you will be paid back with compound interest.

Uh huh. In your dreams, sucker.

Religion isn't the opiate of the people, the conception of justice is. It's our last bastion of rationality, our logical lighthouse on a stormy sea, our anchor. We extend its parameters beyond death—if we haven't found equity in this life, all the great belief systems assure us, just wait until the next. Or the next, or the next. Someday our prince will come.

That may be true, but the paradigm is based on faith, not fact. We can believe in the tooth fairy until the alarm goes off, but unless there's a benevolent parent to value our loss as worth a quarter, we wake up with used calcium, not negotiable currency, under our pillows.

Anthropologists and other social scientists make a distinction between contextual and blind justice. In the former archetype, the goddess has her eyes wide open. It matters—boy, does it matter—who does what to whom, when, how much, and why. In contextual-justice-crazy societies like ours, or like the Yurok of precontact California, rich folks get to pay off their victims, either through a dream team of attorneys or via a prearranged valuation in woodpecker scalps—the murder of an aristocrat worth ever so much more than the slaying of a commoner. If you can afford it, you can do it, and that's the way the game is played. You can't even complain, have begrudging thoughts, or retry the case if the price is right and coughed up in full.

In the theoretical latter case—and is there any manifest and irrefutable instance, really?—it matters not what your station is or what you intended: The act's the thing. All equal before the law. Don't ask, don't tell. A level field, a blank slate. The verdict is impartial and therefore fair. Gripe and you're a sore loser, shortsighted, an excuser of your own incapacities. Strike out and it's because you wanted to in your heart, you didn't wait through the rain, you didn't expend maximum effort. Because if you had, well, you'd wind up—justified. It's a utopian notion, blind justice, an Eden where expectations are perfectly in tune with possibility. But for each of us there comes an undeniable catch, a flaw in the argument. What any human being not convicted of a capital crime has to one day wonder is: What did I do to deserve the death penalty? Be born?

Yet despite the evidence of our private and cultural histories, despite the inevitability of the maximum sentence, when things *don't* work out, we are perpetually surprised. Is this a naiveté carried to an absurd extreme? Wouldn't it be wiser, safer to be shocked at a fleeting *happy* outcome? Wouldn't a pleasant astonishment, however brief, beat bitter disappointment?

But that's too dour. It's downright discouraging. We watch our gritty TV dramas with assurance of retribution, of confirmation. Right prevails, if not this week, then next. Good wins out against all odds. When the innocent victim is convicted on *NYPD Blue* or *Law and Order,* we are outraged; and when the perp goes free, we're appalled. It's not supposed to be that way. We recognize injustice when we see it. We're positively Old Testament in our condemnation. We know how things *should* be.

Our truth. As if it were happening to us.

As it is. All the time.

I've talked to underpaid public defenders, idealistic law school top-ten percenters who chose working within the system over six-figure starting salaries. First year, they're motivated, blessed. Second year, they're cynically busting their chops to spring drug dealers. Third year, they're burnt out, ready for corporate, a health plan, into locking up the very bad guys they've been so busy turning loose. Sellouts, but just ask them and they'll tell you why not. They sleep at night now, go to bed with clear consciences, know what's what, and act on it.

Are their serial analyses accurate? Unless you're an avower of the innate goodness of human nature at twenty-one you'll never be, so use or loose it. Because at thirty you'll know better, you'll have your own kids to protect, you'll be wise to the ways of the world, clear-eyed, maybe even a Republican. Was Kunstler just an old kid, a guy who wouldn't admit harsh facts when they stared him square in the face? Is a $300 suit a give-up buy-in or the minimum salary for up-holding civilization as we know it?

Questions, questions, questions. If we knew the answers or were sure of them we wouldn't have to ask. We yearn to be proven wrong, returned to the innocence of righteous hope. We don't want to be our parents. We want to be as we were: true believers. Please.

We're every generation with a minimal sense of integrity who came before us and reluctantly, partially conceded the fight. We're us. We're our children in twenty years. We're wish. We're further disillusionment waiting to happen.

Do I need examples from "real life" to prove my point? Read the newspaper. Look at world history. Examine your own family. People got what they deserve, right? Oh, really? They didn't?

Okay, call me a downer. There's divine justice, we're assured, a future payday in which everybody knows everything about every-body and rewards and punishments are meted out in precisely the correct quotients. We all stand there on judgment day, quivering, humiliated by our secret transgressions, dreading exposure. There's this apocalyptic division point, like at the Nazi camps: go right, go left. Life, death.

But all that is beside the point, finally. If there's punishment for transgression, that means that order does actually prevail—and the alternative is arguably scarier than hell itself. What if all is chaos and it is simply our own fear, our own cosmological terror, our own instinct as a species to impose structure on whatever we behold? There are scientists who specialize in precisely this kind of bubble-popping on a minor scale: Dr. Amos Tversky, a Stanford University psychologist, working with Dr. Donald Redelmeier, an internist at the University of Toronto, has neatly disproven the long-held tru-ism that people with arthritis can anticipate rainy weather and that a chill brings on a cold; Dr. Albert Kligman, a dermatology profes-sor at the University of Pennsylvania, roundly disproved the widely held notion that eating chocolate exacerbates acne in teenagers. Ac-cording to these and other researchers, human beings innately de-sire predictability and so search out patterns even when there are none. We disregard contrary indications in order to stick firm to our collective wishful thought that events conform to knowable design.

This is the basis, after all, of ritual act. If I do X and Y, then Z will necessarily follow. If once upon a time when I wanted it to rain I sang a certain song at a certain time of day, decked out in a particular outfit, having either eaten or not eaten, had sex or abstained, vocalized or remained silent—and it rained!—then next drought I'd better replicate all the details as precisely as possible. Who knows what caused the moisture to arrive: Was it the sequence? All the ingredients? And if not all, which ones dare I omit? So to be sure, replay, and if the heavens don't open it must have been *my* fault, *I* must have messed up on some aspect. We wear ourselves out in pursuit of the right key to understanding the nature of things, whether we call it physics or witch-doctoring or philosophy. What other sane option is there? If we are ineffectual, if there isn't any grand scheme to discover and plug into, then we're simply spinning wheels. When the sun goes down, it might not rise again. When we go to sleep, we might not wake up. When we die, regardless of whether we've been a sinner or a saint—yikes!

The good news about this impulse of ours is that it begets common assumptions, which are the next best thing to reality. When we give group credence to the same hypotheses we function as if they're absolute, we allow them to define us. When a culture is healthy, cohesive, intellectually homogenous and in sync, we agree that our explanations work—and they seem to. But when we're clustered in a society that's atomized, discordant, at odds, psychological clarity explodes like confetti from a firecracker. If truth is relative, if law is haphazard, if what we term justice is nothing more than occasional and statistical circumstance that we utilize bogusly to reenforce our hope for righteousness, then we dwell not just on a shaky foundation but mired in quicksand.

Not all cultures have grounded their sense of reality in cause-effect relationships. While Genesis postulates a planned, intentionally ordered universe and later books of the Bible stipulate the myriad of rules and regulations we must follow in order to placate, if not please, the divinity, the Nootka Tribe of the Pacific Northwest takes a different approach. In their schema the culture hero is a unisex trickster personified as Raven. Their human creation story goes something like this:

Once, Raven was flying around when it spied a bush loaded with luscious, purple, irresistible berries. Down swoops Raven and gobbles up every one. Finally its breast feathers are stained with juice and its belly is so bloated that it has to get a running start and jump off a cliff to again become airborne. In no time at all, Raven experiences the worst stomach cramps it has ever known, and shortly thereafter a horrible case of diarrhea. It seems to last forever, but when the attack is over, Raven breathes a sigh of relief and looks down to the earth to see the mess it has made. And there we are!

In the Nootka cosmology, justice, like much else, is chance not ordained. Things simply happen without structure or divine plan. The proper response to the tale—and to the organization of the world that it implies—is laughter rather than smugness or indignation. Don't expect from me, the universe seems to suggest, but don't blame me either. You're on your own.

An interesting notion, but we in the West are programmed to content ourselves with being appalled, insisting that we're stunned when injustice seems to triumph. The *human*-created system has broken down, we persuade ourselves. This is but a temporary aberration. Just hold out for the eventual guaranteed happy ending. Cling to the Beatitudes and the meek *will* inherit the earth. Be like Pascal and choose to behave as if we're sure in our convictions, betting that if, God forbid, we're wrong, we'll never have to find out. Like the ground beneath the circling trickster, we'll never know what hit us.

GARRETT HONGO

HR 442: REDRESS

In April 1988, I was in the Senate gallery on hand for what I expected to be the final floor debate and passage of HR 442, legislation devised to compensate Japanese American survivors of the World War II relocation program. The idea was for the government to issue a formal apology and pay a financial settlement to anyone living who had suffered the forced evacuation and internment during World War II. Ceremoniously, the bill took its name after the all-Nisei Combat Team that had won numerous decorations for heroism on the battlefields of both Italy and France.

By now, everybody knows the story: How, in the aftermath of the Japanese bombing of Pearl Harbor in Hawaii, President Franklin Roosevelt signed Executive Order 9066, sending 120,000 Japanese Americans into camps surrounded by barbed wire and run by the military, far removed from any populated areas; how these Americans were unjustly accused of disloyalty; how the action was a result of racial prejudice and wartime hysteria; and how a good bunch of people were made to suffer greatly. Yet before the passage of HR 442, these facts were known mainly within the Japanese American community; the general public's attitude about them was either one of indifference, denial, or even mild hostility. Moreover, Japanese Americans themselves had to overcome their own powerful feelings of shame and fear that had remained from those times.

On the afternoon just before the bill's final passage, I was upstairs in the balcony overlooking the Senate floor, listening to a mannerly but nettlesome debate between Spark Matsunaga from Hawaii and Jesse Helms of North Carolina. Matsunaga, as its author, had been taking the measure through debate, all largely tributary. But, at the last minute, Jesse Helms had proposed an unfriendly "Pearl Harbor Amendment."

Though Helms agreed that history, in its twenty-twenty hindsight, has shown that the evacuation and relocation was a mistake, he still wanted an amendment to stipulate that no funds be appropriated until the Japanese government compensated the families of the men and women who were killed at Pearl Harbor on December 7, 1941.

"I owe this to the families of our military personnel at Pearl Harbor who were either killed or injured," Helms was saying, pitting redress against memories of America's war dead.

We were still being associated with Japanese war atrocities. My own grandfather, American-born, had been imprisoned for a time because of this kind of prejudice, and my father, all of seventeen then, had shipped out in 1944 as part of a contingent to replace Nisei troops lost in European combat. Despite all this, Helms could still put us back into the frame of that old story. It was the Japanese American version of the Scottsboro Boys.

I thought about this for a while, glancing at the others sitting with me in the gallery that afternoon. There were a couple of dozen other Japanese Americans from different parts of the country. They represented three generations: Nisei, second-generation; Sansei, third-generation; and Yonsei, fourth-generation. And they all had something to do with redress. We were quiet, waiting to hear how Senator Matsunaga would reply.

Matsunaga, now deceased, was over seventy then, and the issue on which this bill was based had been an important one to him for a long time. He had been a lieutenant in the army during World War II and saw combat in Italy, fighting alongside other Japanese American soldiers whose families were imprisoned in the United States.

His colleague and cosponsor of the bill, Hawaii Senator Daniel Inouye, had been through a similar experience, losing an arm in combat. They were American war heroes. Even Senator Helms, speaking
in opposition to the bill, had to acknowledge this. He referred to
their military service, their "valor," and made protestations about
how much he respected them.

Up in the gallery, I had been hoping for the scene below to add
up to a closing moment. For over ten years a "redress movement"
had been building along several fronts. It pushed to educate the
American public about the internment of Japanese Americans,
pushed for federal legislation to grant monetary compensation, and
petitioned the courts to overturn old Supreme Court cases that upheld the legality of the evacuation order of 1942.

In April 1984, a federal district court in San Francisco had
granted a special *coram nobis* petition brought by a team of young
Japanese American attorneys. They had asked that the case known
as *United States v. Korematsu* be set aside, that Fred Korematsu, a
Nisei who had been convicted for refusing to comply with the
evacuation order in 1942, be declared innocent and his record ex-
punged. The new federal decision did that. Subsequently, in 1986,
a district judge in Seattle ruled favorably in the matter of another
coram nobis petition regarding *United States v. Hirabayashi,* a similar
1942 Supreme Court case. These were historic victories for the
Japanese American community and personal ones for the two
Nisei men then convicted for refusing to obey the evacuation or-
ders. The cases galvanized community and media attention, educated the public, and gave Japanese Americans at large a feeling of
vindication.

In October 1987, the National History Museum of the Smith-
sonian Institute had opened a major exhibit, scheduled for perpet-
ual display, entitled "A More Perfect Union: Japanese Americans
and the U.S. Constitution." It dramatized both the evacuation itself
and the heroic war contributions of Japanese American soldiers,
spotlighting national media attention on what had been an almost
forgotten episode and made a case against the government for the
World War II civil rights violations of its Japanese American

citizens. Thousands of Japanese Americans from all over the country had converged on Washington for a series of public ceremonies, reunions, and private receptions commemorating the event.

Finally, and perhaps most significantly, a push for federal legislation grew out of a long-term exercise in American democracy—something the Japanese American community had, ever since the war years, a collectively troubled belief in. For over a decade, there had been a tempestuous political campaign run from within the membership of the Japanese American Citizens' League (JACL), a national political organization, by former evacuees like Edison Uno, Min Yasui, and John Tateishi who wanted to push Congress to make official amends for the internment years. Uno, a Nisei on the education faculty at San Francisco State University, had long been an activist in the cause to accomplish some restitution to Japanese Americans for what they had suffered. During the late 1960s and throughout the 1970s, Uno had come repeatedly to lobby the JACL National Convention to introduce a resolution asking that the U.S. government provide reparations to Japanese Americans.

In 1970 Uno drafted a resolution calling for the government to make an official apology and to pay monetary compensation, and thereby authored what had become the two fundamental tenets of Japanese American redress. Given the Elizabethan-sounding title of "A Requital Supplication," Uno's resolution became the focus for a national campaign within the JACL. But the membership remained bitterly divided about the issue for eight more years. There were many who still suffered from great psychological turmoil and social fears from their years in the internment camps. They found it hard to even mention those times, much less push Congress for any significant legislation.

"They really had been thinking of themselves as second-class citizens," said John Tateishi, who became the inheritor of the movement Uno had started. A well-spoken and smartly dressed man, Tateishi is the Sansei, a third-generation Japanese American, who became National Chairman of the JACL Redress Committee in 1976. I spoke to him at a reception sponsored by the National History Museum.

"The Nisei were reluctant. It took a lot of discussion amongst ourselves. A *process* had to take place. People needed to voice reservations. They had to focus on the issue of our acceptance as citizens in this country. They had to face the fact that they really had been thinking of themselves as *second-class* and conquer that sense, quite deep-rooted, within themselves. They had to come out of a profound dread of bringing back the psychological pain. These were people who couldn't even talk to their wives or husbands about the internment, not to mention their kids."

Grace Uyehara, a Nisei social worker from Philadelphia, served with Tateishi on the Redress Committee and eventually succeeded him as National Coordinator. A smallish woman in her seventies, she echoed some of his observations when I spoke to her.

"We were raised not to expose feelings," she said to me over coffee in a Washington restaurant. "Do you know *haji?*" She used the Japanese word for "shame."

"We felt something must've been wrong with *us,* that we were the unwanted people. It was hard for us to admit we were a despised people, a rejected people," she told me. "That was the toughest. After that, we had to create the network and realize we had a responsibility to change the direction of our society—not only American society, but the direction *within* the Japanese American community. We had some unfinished business to attend to. The resolution forced us to deal with the feeling that it wasn't *us,* but that it was American society that was wrong."

The Salt Lake City JACL Convention in 1978 passed a two-part resolution calling for a governmental apology and a financial payment to survivors. It asked that $25,000 be paid to each individual who went through the internment. The demand of the $25,000 drew immediate media attention. The JACL began attracting wider public attention to the issue. Overall, even though the membership remained regionally and politically fractured, the resolution itself created a public sense that there was now a unified voice coming out of Japanese America.

In January 1979, armed with their resolution, officials from the JACL finally approached the Nikkei Caucus for help in devising a scheme for accomplishing legislation. The Nikkei Caucus referred to the small group of four Japanese American legislators then in Washington. It was made up of Senators Matsunaga and Inouye of Hawaii and Representatives Norman Mineta and Robert Matsui of California. The legislation was personally important to each of them. Matsunaga said, "I had relatives who were confined in those camps." Mineta and Matsui had, as children, both been victims of the wartime internment. "I owe it to my buddies," Inouye had said, gesturing to a battalion flag in the corner of his Senate office.

The group met many times over a four-month period and assessed the difficulty of introducing such legislation without any other preparation than the JACL resolution. Senator Daniel Inouye proposed an idea to create a commission that would study the matter and hold public hearings throughout the country. By thus exposing the issue to national and local media, they hoped to gather support for the Japanese American point of view. The committee would then give a final report to the House Judiciary Committee and make official recommendations. Perhaps one of those recommendations would be for legislation.

When I visited Senator Inouye in his Senate office back in 1987, he emphasized planning and consensus-building.

"A massive education job was necessary," Inouye said. "The majority of Americans are only vaguely aware of what happened to Japanese Americans during World War II."

Many colleagues in the Senate were also ignorant. "I tried to convince them by speaking to each one personally," Matsunaga told me. "They didn't know! Not being of Japanese ancestry or close to anyone who was, it took some time to explain it to them."

"I was convinced," Inouye said, "that if we came up with a measure *flat out,* it would not be accepted. In order to make it succeed, it had to be a national effort, not just an effort pursued by Americans of Japanese ancestry. So I suggested that the commission be made up not of Japanese Americans but of a cross-section of distinguished Americans. It would be a weak case if it was just a movement supported by one narrow segment of our community. This had to be a national effort. It had to be a recommendation coming from the people of the United States saying clearly that a wrong had been committed against a small segment of Americans and that something should be done about it. I thought that approach would be better than a Japanese American group saying 'They have done us wrong, therefore you owe us something, and therefore you should do something for us.' And so you pit a small group against a nation. Now, this other way, the nation is coming out and saying, 'You picked on that small group. You shouldn't have done that.' "

The Inouye strategy was implemented. According to Mineta, it took two Congresses, but the Presidential Commission on Wartime Relocation and Internment of Civilians completed its work in June 1983, having conducted numerous public hearings throughout the West Coast and in Washington, D.C. It heard testimony from scores of citizens who had been interned during the war. These people spoke repeatedly and with great emotion about their experiences, many of them for the first time in their lives. The hearings were a momentous and catalytic event for the Japanese American community, and, for the first time since the evacuation of 1942, a story about them was making national and local news.

The Commission's report to the House Judiciary Committee in December 1982 was a spectacular victory for the redress movement. Given the suggestive title "Personal Justice Denied," the report stated that the wartime internment not only was unwarranted but was a result of "race prejudice, war hysteria and a failure of political leadership." It described suffering and deprivation in tar-paper barracks, mass living in conditions that humiliated and prevented normal family intimacy. The Commission's recommendations urged that redress be legislated and that a sum of $20,000 be paid to each survivor.

The Nikkei Caucus then busied itself lining up support within both houses of Congress. Over the next five years, a team of lobbyists from the JACL joined with them, recruiting into the cause Members like Dick Cheney and Jim Wright, Senators like Bill Bradley. "We made it an issue of national honor," Matsunaga said.

Under the leadership of Speaker Jim Wright, the 100th Congress ceremoniously passed redress legislation on the day of the

Constitutional Bicentennial, September 17, 1987. Democratic leaders like Tom Foley, Tony Coelho, and Barney Frank had fought for it, and, when it came to the House floor for discussion, some of the speeches given in support were poetic tributes and lyric testimonies.

"I would like . . . to indicate to all of you perhaps what it was like to be an American citizen in 1942 if you happened to be of Japanese ancestry," Congressman Matsui had said. "My mother and father who were in their twenties were both born and raised in Sacramento, California, so they were American citizens by birth. They were trying to start their careers. They had a child who was six months old. They had a home like any other American. They had a car. My father had a little produce business with his brother. For some reason because of Pearl Harbor in 1942, their lives and their futures were shattered. They were given 72 hours' notice that they had to leave their home, their neighborhood, abandon their business, and show up at the Memorial Auditorium which is in the heart of Sacramento and then be taken, like cattle in trains, to the Tule Lake Internment Camp. My father was not able to talk about this subject for over forty years. . . . I was a six-month-old child born in this country."

Norman Mineta chose to read a letter his father had written from an internment camp to friends, describing what he felt as he left his home.

"I looked at Santa Clara's streets from the train over the subway," Mineta said, quoting his father. "I thought this might be the last look at my loved home city. My heart almost broke, and suddenly hot tears came pouring out, and the whole family cried out, could not stop, until we were out of our loved country." Mineta had wept and his voice choked as he read. "We lost our homes, we lost our businesses, we lost our farms," the Congressman said in summation, "but worst of all we lost our basic human rights."

When the roll call vote was taken, redress had passed the House 243–141.

Within the Senate, Matsunaga had introduced a similar bill and signed on seventy-six cosponsors, including Republican conservatives

Orrin Hatch, Alan Simpson, and Ted Stevens. "He made this almost a personal crusade," his colleague Inouye told me. Fellow Democrats like John Glenn, Paul Simon, and Alan Cranston also helped give the bill its avid bipartisan support. Though it was originally scheduled immediately after passage of the House bill, the Senate's version of redress came up for discussion in April of the following year. At the time, Matsunaga worried briefly about a threat of filibustering from Jesse Helms. A vote for cloture, a procedure to limit discussion to forty-eight hours, prevented this, however, and insured that opposition would not be effective.

But in the Senate gallery that afternoon, I could still feel an atmosphere of worry. Helms's opposition still struck a nerve. I felt the specter of an old fear.

In the first row was Mike Masaoka, a deeply tanned and gray-haired Nisei man in his seventies. At the time of the war, Masaoka was National Secretary of the Japanese American Citizens' League, a kind of national Kiwanis Club or NAACP for Japanese Americans. After Pearl Harbor, he was one of a few Japanese American leaders called in to meet with officials from the Roosevelt administration. Masaoka, then in his late twenties, had publicly urged compliance with the relocation order.

"We were misled by the government," he had told me when I spoke to him. "We were desperate, you see. If the army was going to move us out, if they had to come in with bayonets, what would be the reaction of the American people? We decided to cooperate rather than have the army come after us. We sat down, we tried to work it out thinking that the more we cooperated with them, the more livable they'd make things in camp. It was a question of survival then."

Listening to Masaoka speak then, I found myself feeling empathetic with his anxieties. It is deeply ingrained among many minorities that we will not be understood, that our truths will never be part of the national truth, that we are still second-class. It has ensured our silence about injustice many times. It was clear to me that Masaoka had felt powerless in 1942, called before Congress and to private meetings with the military as a leader of the Japanese American community that, as a whole, was under powerful suspicion.

"I keep looking over the facts, over and over again. I talked to the generals, the FBI agents, and other people whom we cooperated with, and I'm convinced that the alternative would have been disastrous. We would have had absolutely no future in this country."

Redress, for Masaoka and others, was a way to get the story told right, the political means to accomplish a wish, said over and again, that the evacuation and relocation episode *be known,* that the story no longer be confined within our own community.

"I want the American people to understand what happened to us," Masaoka said. "I want our history written down."

Helms's misplaced jingoism stood in the way. He rose from his desk on the Senate floor, finishing his statements.

"I have heard from a lot of survivors of American fighting men who were killed in Pearl Harbor on December 7, 1941, and they say, 'How about us?'" Helms said.

But there was a new story out there about Japanese Americans now, and the Senator from North Carolina seemed to be the only one still trying to tell the old one.

"This amendment is totally unacceptable," Senator Matsunaga replied. "It presumes that we Americans of Japanese ancestry had something to do with the bombing of Pearl Harbor. That is absolutely false. In this bill we are trying to distinguish between Japanese Americans and Japanese. The amendment would obscure this distinction."

Matsunaga had said it forcefully, succinctly. Behind his statements were all his accomplishments, the Nikkei Caucus, the emotional speeches of scores of his colleagues already made on the House and Senate floors endorsing the bill, and, finally, about ten years of a national political movement.

It was over. Matsunaga and Helms, both standing, locked eyes, and then Helms dropped back into his seat, mopping his brow with a handkerchief. Matsunaga remained standing. A motion to table Helms's "Pearl Harbor Amendment" passed 91–4.

The roll call vote followed. A buzzer went off, and the entire Senate assembled. One by one, from Bill Bradley, the most athletic, to Howard Metzenbaum, the most stooped, Senators glided and shuffled to the voting table at the front of the hall. Inouye and Matsunaga stood alongside one another and shook hands with everyone. After the announcement of the final vote (69–27), Matsunaga grabbed Inouye's hand and raised it with his. Old-timers, they blew sentimental aloha kisses to the Nisei gallery.

I was full of my own dreamy sentimentalisms then, trying to rhapsodize myself into the emotional center of this story. When I spoke with the pool of newspaper reporters later, I was critical of their descriptions of Senator Matsunaga as a kind of American Don Quixote finalizing a crusade, achieving his dream. I said that the characterization was too romantic: "It implies impossibility." Borrowing a phrase from a poem of Coleridge's, I said what Matsunaga had done was more like maintaining "a quiet ministry of faith."

The next day, I read my remarks as leads from syndicated news stories in Knight-Rider, Gannett, and Copley News Service papers all over America.

"Passage of this bill has freed me from a burden I've carried for over forty years," Congressman Matsui told me not long afterwards. "It just *had* to be done."

When I left the Senate late in the afternoon, a wonderful light drizzled down through all the trees on the street outside. Redress had brought about a transformation of awareness in the national consciousness about Japanese Americans. The movement had successfully established their innocence and loyalty during World War II and refocused public opinion. Finally, the unique legislation accomplished by Matsunaga and the Nikkei Caucus was evidence that, after almost half a century, the official story about the evacuation and internment, one that had been clouded in fear, shame, and suspicion, had finally been corrected.

"It's all over," said Matsui. "We can talk about it. It's no longer something we should be ashamed of."

CHARLES JOHNSON

EXECUTIVE DECISION

Act as if the principle of thy action were to become by thy will a universal law of nature.
KANT, *FUNDAMENTAL PRINCIPLES OF THE METAPHYSIC OF MORALS*

Put simply, your task is impossible.

There are two names short-listed for the position your company has advertised. These two have surfaced as the most appealing candidates after a six-month search that left you and your Seattle staff red-eyed and exhausted after sifting through the files of more than eight hundred applicants, and phoning dozens of references, some of them as far away as southern France and Osaka. You've met their spouses, their children. Read their personal statements. Called them back for second interviews. Probed into their after-hours interests, taken them to dinner, and now you, and you alone—as the grandson of the company's founder—must decide. Naturally, both are being wooed by other businesses and by government. If you delay the decision any longer, you will lose them to a competitor. So by 9 A.M. tomorrow the six-figure job, with its benefits and stock options, must be awarded to either Claire Bennett or Eddie Childs, and the other given an apology.

It is the most troublesome decision of your life.

Imprimis: You are a man who, though quite radical in your youth, has come to see the wisdom in not rocking the boat overly much if advocacy means the ship might take on too much water, its hull give way, and its many passengers—employees, stockholders, and their families—disappear beneath the briny. If nothing else, a life in business has so instilled in you the value of prudence that even your closest friends from college remark how dull and safe, portly and bald you've become since the days you marched arm-in-arm with civil rights workers through the streets of Cambridge. Yet and still, in your personal and professional affairs alike, you have always believed in fairness, though on some occasions precisely what *is* fair seems elusive. The question was so much clearer in the black-and-white time of youth. Not long after your father became ill and the company passed into your hands thirty years ago, you insisted in board meetings that the Personnel Department aggressively seek out blacks and women.

It was an outrageous thing to do in 1966, but then you were fresh out of Harvard, with a degree in philosophy (partly to spite your parents), having focused on epistemology, the problems of appearances vs. reality; two arrests for demonstrating on campus, with the oratory of Martin Luther King Jr.—"Power at its best is love implementing the demands of justice; justice at its best is love correcting everything that stands against love"—still echoing in your ears. At first your only supporter was old Gladys McNeal, your father's personal secretary, factotum, and possibly his lover as well. She is your secretary now—a precise, never-married woman who could pass for actress Estelle Getty's sister, though Gladys won't talk about her age and has never uttered a word about her family. She'd called your fight to hire more minorities and women "brave." And eventually, the company acquiesced to your wishes, placing more blacks on the custodial staff and women in the secretarial pool in the late '60s and early '70s, and a sprinkling of both in middle management during the '80s.

Lately some of the black employees have been grumbling to you and Gladys about the absence of African Americans in the firm's administrative wing. (Gladys only nods when the subject comes up and looks away, knowing they're right.) You can see them at their desks through the glass walls that separate their tiny, cluttered work stations from your spacious chamber (with its carpeted floors and plaster-of-paris bust of Cicero) and those of your two chief executives, old friends whom to this very day you still affectionately call by their fraternity nicknames, Turk and Nips—it's dyspeptic, eccentric old Turk who's retiring due to poor health and whose position Bennett and Childs hope to fill.

Except for a black janitor, the top-floor office in your downtown building on Fifth and Pine is empty at 10 P.M. You have stayed behind to review the candidates' qualifications and your notes one last time. Their files—thicker than the white pages for Wenatchee—are spread out on your desk beneath the glow of the handcrafted lamp given to you as a birthday gift from your wife Emilie, a painter who could not resist this high-end item that translates Monet's *Water Lilies* into five hundred multicolored glass panels on its triangular shade. In the light of this lamp, you pour over these pages, looking for the one fact or feeling that might edge one of these candidates ahead of the other. To your great perplexity, both look equally qualified—or, if not exactly matched, what you see as deficiencies in one are balanced by a strength the other does not possess.

But except before the law, and in the eyes of God, are *any* two people truly equal?

Claire, you recall, was forthcoming and full of wonderfully funny stories during her first three-hour interview. She was a graduate of Boston University. Even before you, Turk, and Nips sat her down in the conference room, with its breathtaking view of snow-capped Mt. Rainier in the background, the four of you were swapping stories about your undergraduate days and New England associates you had in common. It was as if you'd known her all your life. She felt at home in the Northwest, having grown up in Portland, where her parents sent her to Catlin Gabel, a private school dating back to 1870, and one of the best independent academies in the region. Her parents, both professionals, provided her with private tutors, a course in modeling when she was fourteen (afraid she was awkward and unlovely), and trips with her father to Barcelona, Paris, and Tokyo when his work required that he travel (her Japanese was flawless). Despite an early struggle with epilepsy, which she controlled with Clonopin, Claire graduated from college near the top of her class, accepted her first job with a firm in Chicago, and, after several early promotions, found herself positioned as the assistant to the company's CEO when disaster stuck in the form of a class-action suit against the firm. That, she explained, taught her more than anything she'd learned in college. Claire put out fires, she controlled the damage, and learned firsthand the meaning of a saying she'd heard when traveling in the Far East, "In chaos there is also opportunity."

During her interview, she was relaxed, laughed easily, and scored points when she said, "I see my *first* job as being the protection of the company." She was 28 years old, six-feet-two in her heels, and wore her corn-colored hair to her shoulders. And did she have faults? Nips felt Claire had slightly more nose than she needed. And he noticed that rather than completely agreeing with the things he said, she prefaced her replies by saying, "Yes, but . . . " and "Oh, it's *more* than that, of course . . . " Furthermore, she had done her homework and was aware of the company's history, its strengths and weaknesses, and guided her interview to such an extent that it seemed *they,* not she, who were being looked over and scrutinized. That Nips didn't enjoy. On the other hand, Turk liked it just fine.

Claire's husband Bill, a shaggy, bearded, Old English sheepdog of a fellow with hair falling into his brown eyes, came along for her second interview; he was self-employed—a moderately successful sculptor ("installation artist" was the term he preferred)—and could relocate with no difficulty if she got the job. He'd surprised you when, after shambling into your office in a corduroy jacket and jeans, he shook your hand firmly (his palm was rough, toughened like that of a carpenter), then paused to look at the lamp, and nodded in approval. "Nice, that's a reproduction of Louis Comfort Tiffany's work, isn't it? The bronze patina on the base places the design somewhere in the twenties . . . "

That you hadn't known—the lamp's history—but you and Emilie were pretty sure of this: You liked the Bennetts. Emilie called them "people persons." And so they were. Their ten-year-old daughter, a bright, brown-skinned girl named Nadia, was Filipino—

their own child, a boy, had died from SIDS—and Nadia was the first of two or three children the Bennetts hoped to adopt. If you hired Claire, you knew she would not only protect the interests of your business as if it were her own, but her family and yours might become the best of friends. Added to which, and perhaps most important of all, she would be the first woman to break through the company's "glass ceiling," which was definitely a plus in the present, gender-charged political climate.

But then there was Childs . . .

He was thirty-one, from a large, Atlanta family—four boys, five girls—and the first member of his family to graduate from college (Morehouse) after serving in the navy. On the day of his interview he looked trim and fit in his three-piece suit: a dark-skinned man with close-cropped hair, a thin moustache like movie star David Niven's, and nails more neatly manicured than your own. When he answered a question, or a series of them put to him by Nips and Turk, Childs always turned to look directly at the person who'd asked it, never forgetting who'd originated the query. But unlike Claire, even when he appeared at ease you saw that Childs never completely relaxed. In high school, he confessed, a white teacher told him that he'd never be college material and directed him toward a blue-collar trade. "That woke me up," Childs said. "He made me so mad I guess I've been fighting to prove him wrong since I was fifteen years old."

You saw in Childs the attitude of a man who believed nothing would ever come to him easily, that he had to work twice as hard as others to get half as far—and four times that to break even. And so he had. He'd made his own opportunities. His record showed he'd worked full-time as a nightwatchman while attending Morehouse, studying and saving and having, he said, no social life at all. After college, he returned to Atlanta and started his own business from scratch, one he later sold, but not before Childs paid off the mortgage on his parents' home, and put one of his siblings through school. He was actively involved in his church, the NAACP, and a community group dedicated to helping at-risk youth. His references included half a dozen names in Atlanta's city government and two black congressmen. He had nothing to say about the lamp on your desk, but what he and his wife Leslie, an elementary school teacher, knew firsthand and through research about this country's marginalized history—the contributions from people of color—stunned you, Turk, and Nips into respectful yet nervous silence.

You listened carefully to what he said.

You learned that blacks suffered twice the unemployment rate of whites and earned only half as much (56 percent); that a decade ago they comprised 7 percent of professionals, 5 percent of managers, 8 percent of technicians, 11 percent of service workers, and 41 percent of domestic workers. There were, he told you, 620,912 black-owned businesses, but 47 percent of them had gross annual receipts of less than $5,000. For every 1,000 Arabs, 108 owned a business; for every 1,000 Asians, it was 96; for every 1,000 whites, 64, and for every 1,000 blacks, the number was 9. Worse, the typical black household had a net worth less than one-tenth that of white households. AIDS among black Americans was six times the rate it was for whites, and every four hours a young black male died from gunfire. Seventy percent of black children were born to single mothers; 57 percent were in fatherless homes, which was more than double the 21 percent for whites. This was the background of poverty and inequality Eddie and Leslie Childs had survived—a world in which black men in the early '90s accounted for half those murdered in America; they had less chance of reaching age sixty-five than men in Bangladesh. One out of three were in prison (the number was 827,440 in 1995) or on parole. It was a world where, as Childs put it, quoting Richard Pryor, justice was known simply as "just us." Given these staggering obstacles, you are amazed this man is even alive.

Little wonder then during his visit he never seemed to relax, or let his hair down, or get too comfortable. You, Turk, and Nips were not sure he would ever completely trust you or, for that matter, much of anything in this world. But despite his admiration for this couple, Turk had reservations about Childs. After dinner he'd asked the candidate over to his home to join your Friday night poker game, and Childs politely declined, saying, "I would prefer not to. I don't play cards." He confessed, "My wife is always saying I'm not much of a fun person. All I do is work." Yes, he was formal, guarded, and, even after two interview sessions, opaque. He was—what word do you want?—*different*. Sometimes you did not understand his humor. You certainly did not know his heart—*that* would come slowly, perhaps even painfully if you presumed too much about him, and it might be hard at first, a challenge, with you tripping lightly, walking on eggs around him until everyone in the office eased into familiarity. Was one candidate worth all that work? In his interview, Childs outlined two strategies for improving diversity in personnel and ideas for better marketing the firm's product to minorities who, he emphasized, would be in the minority no longer after the coming millennium. Nips felt he was right, but naturally *he* would, being never satisfied with the way things were in the world (including the desk in his office, which he was forever rearranging and replacing). In the morning he was always a little dull, possibly hung-over (for Nips still enjoyed visiting night spots where he met, he said, people from numerous walks of life); but as the day progressed, and he slowly sobered, his disposition generally improved. The country's demographics were changing, Nips said. All you had to do was walk out your door to see that. If the company hoped to survive into the twenty-first century, a multiracial arrangement was needed. He cast his vote categorically for Childs, and asked you and Turk to do the same.

But Turk would not budge on Bennett.

"Why discuss this any further?" he said, after Bennett returned to Chicago and Childs to Atlanta. Between the three of you a bottle of scotch from the bottom drawer of your filing cabinet was passed around, Nips drinking from a papercup, Turk from a coffee mug imprinted with the insignia of the Seahawks. He'd made his decision by 7 P.M., but Turk was notorious for being a morning person, and you seldom trusted anything he said or did after lunch when his vitality was low, his round face flushed pink, his manner rude, and his judgments often dubious. "Bennett will be good for the operation, especially overseas. As reliable, I believe, as old Gladys. I think she can weather any crisis that comes along, make us a lot of money,

and keep the stockholders happy. That's all *I* need to know." He
chuckled into his mug. "She's no Nicholas Leeson."

"Who?" you asked.

"The British kid who brought down Baring Brothers and Company. You remember, don't you? The company was two hundred
and thirty-two years old. It helped finance the Napoleanic wars.
Lord knows how it happened, but they made Leeson manager of
their Singapore office, and he gambled that the Tokyo market
would go up. Turns out, it went down, and 800 million of Baring's
money with it." Turk laughed again, wickedly. "I *love* that story.
Just shows you what can happen, if you hire wrong."

"But," asked Nips, "does Bennett *deserve* the job more than
Childs?"

Turk's face tightened in a frown.

"How's that again—deserve, I heard you say? We have a job to
offer, and it's ours to extend or withhold as we see fit. We may hire
or fire the most qualified employee, as legal scholar Richard Epstein
puts it, for good reason, bad reason, or no reason at all."

"And you think that's prudent?"

"I think it's practical, yes. And perfectly within our rights."

"You are not," pressed Nips, "concerned about discrimination?"

"Oh, shaw! We *all* discriminate, Nips! Every moment of every
day we choose one thing rather than another on the basis of our tastes,
prejudices, and preferences. How *else* can we pursue Life, Liberty, and
the Pursuit of Happiness? I remember that *you,* back in our school
days, never deigned to direct your affections toward women taller
than yourself or, for that matter, toward men. It's reasonable, I'm saying, to have likes and dislikes, and to act upon them, to prefer this
over that because, for heaven's sake, no two things in nature are the
same. Really, man, be realistic. The Japanese don't spend a moment
agonizing over things like this, and look how they trumped us in the
eighties! Preferential policies have weakened this nation's GNP. And
just *how* is one to decide *whom* to prefer when not only blacks but His-
panics, Native Americans, and twenty-eight varieties of Asians are
listed as preferred by the federal government?"

Nips listened patiently, as he always did when Turk, slightly in his cups, tilted toward the pomp and preachment of a Thrasymachus. He nodded in agreement, "Racial categories *do* cause a lot of confusion." For a few moments he said nothing, hoping, no doubt, that you and Turk would ponder the stories reported about whites with only a fraction of Mexican or Indian blood who invoked a distant minority in their family tree to qualify for the government's set-aside programs.

Then quietly, he asked, "Do you remember that class we took with John Rawls?"

"Vaguely, yes. I nearly flunked it. Had something to do with the state being like a joint-stock company. A lot of Hobbes and Locke rehashed, if I recall it rightly."

"There was more to it than that. He said when justice is seen as fairness, men of unequal circumstances agree to share one another's fate. Social advantage and native endowment of any sort—whether they be inherited wealth, talent, beauty, or imagination—are undeserved. They are products of the arbitrariness of fortune. But Rawls did not say we must eradicate these inequities, only adjust them so the least favored benefit too. If the fortunate do not share, then the least advantaged have every right to break the social contract that has so miserably failed to serve their needs. They riot. They rebel. Without the cooperation of the least favored, the social order collapses for *everyone.*"

"I remember you did well in that course—"

"Better than you because in my final paper I argued that it is in the interest of the favored to redress the damage caused by slavery and a century of segregation."

"Wronged by *whom*? Nips, I can assure you *I* had nothing to do with with it. All that happened before our time!"

"Then we have *no* greater social obligations?"

"My dear friend," Turk patted Nips on his knee, "making the monthly payroll on time so employees and their families are not unduly inconvenienced is, in my humble opinion, social obligation enough. I am for the candidate who puts *that* first."

"Be honest," said Nips, "you're just not comfortable with colored people, are you?"

"That's hardly fair! I can't *say*, because I don't know any!"

"Exactly my point."

They argued that way for most of the evening, through three
bottles of whiskey, long after Gladys clicked off the lights in the
outer office (she pretty much ran the place, knew where all the bodies were buried, and was always the first employee to arrive and the
last to leave). Turk and Nips staggered out together, carrying their
disagreement into the hallway and elevator, neither of them willing
to support the other's candidate for the job.

It falls to you to break the tie.

Come midnight, you are still torn, divided within as if you were
two people, or perhaps three. No question that these candidates are
antinomies. But what, then, is the just decision? Could there be
color-blind decisions in a country wracked by race? Or was Turk
correct that it was not a question of racial justice at all? All night
you have worried this question into mere words, a blur of sound sig-
nifying, it seems, nothing. And now it is too late to catch the last
ferry home to Whidbey Island. Emilie no doubt has already tucked
the children in bed and turned in for the night. After taking off
your suitcoat, kicking off your shoes, pulling loose your tie and top
button, you run water into the coffee maker, then wearily plop
down on the black leather sofa, rubbing your face with both hands.
You spread the files on the coffee table, staring at them for another
hour. A *black* man. A *white* woman. No. That was wrong. These
empty signifiers had names, faces, specific histories that exploded
sterile sociological categories and rendered both candidates ineffa-
ble and inexhaustible in their individuality. Their portfolios provided no clues whatsoever to their promise, or to unkeying the para-
dox of justice. Wearily, you push them away, close your eyes, and
drift in and out of sleep until sunlight brightens the room and,
below the office window, night's silence swells with the sound of
morning traffic.

Gladys opens the outer door at 8 A.M. Her key in the latch sends
you hurrying in your stocking feet to the bathroom and closet

adjacent to your chamber. After splashing water on your face and brushing your teeth with two fingers, you reach into the closet where you keep a few fresh shirts still encased in crackling plastic from the cleaners. This is where your father kept his extra shirts and ties. It's where you played sometimes as a child, hiding in the closet when he dictated letters to Gladys. Four decades ago she'd been heartbreakingly beautiful, a brunette with bee-stung lips and eyes so green, so light, you wondered if she could really see through them. That she was quiet yet gentle, always smiling ironically as if she had a secret, never talked about herself, or her relations in New Orleans, or what she did away from the office only added an element of mystery to the gaps in what one knew personally about her. You suppose a man like your father could fill that with all manner of fantasies if his marriage was stale, his duties heavy, and he believed, rightly or wrongly, that her secrets could heal. Your mother was the one who'd told you these things, but not angrily because she had several affairs of her own. In fact, she'd seemed as amused by the brevity of your father's only midlife fling as by his choice.

Around your throat the shirt's top button strains, a sign you're getting fatter at fifty-one. You're about to swear when something happens outside in your office that stops you cold. Someone is whistling a few bars from "Uptown Downbeat," an Ellington tune, one of your father's favorites. Walking to the bathroom's partly opened door, you see Gladys tidying up the files you left on the coffee table. Her hair, once obsidian and shiny, curls round her head in a cap of gray when she removes her rainbow-colored scarf. Believing herself to be alone in the office, she does a little dance step, snapping her fingers, shaking her hips, and for a flickerflash instant she seems as young, as beautiful as Halle Berry.

Different.

Then she notices you, abruptly stops dancing, and, after composing herself—she is Estelle Getty again—steps to the window and opens the curtains, flooding the room with sunlight.

"You didn't spend the night here again, did you?" For years she's spoken like that, the way a doting godmother would. It takes you a moment to find your voice.

"Afraid so."

"Would you like me to put on some coffee?"

"Please."

You watch her leave, understanding only now why she looked away when the blacks in middle management complained there were no Negroes in administration. How had Nips put it? Categories were chimerical. Mere constructs. When she comes back, carrying a carafe filled with water and a bag of Starbucks, you try not to stare or seem too confounded that Gladys is black. Or is she? By all appearances, she is as white as you.

"Gladys," clearing your throat, "you met both Bennett and Childs. Which one would you feel best about hiring?"

She pauses, cupping the carafe in both hands. "Is this a trick question?"

"No, honestly, which one?"

"Well, I liked them both, but—"

"But what?"

"Oh, it's nothing, just that Mr. Childs reminds me of Mr. Turk when he was hired. Neither was very much at ease. And I know your father never approved of Mr. Turk. His references weren't that good, if I remember, or his grades, but he got the job because he was your friend and you insisted. You acted in his behalf, and that was all right." She smiles and you see Halle Berry again; then, as the muscles around her mouth relax, Estelle Getty. "These matters are never neutral, are they?"

"No . . . I'd forgotten. . . ."

"And people are not what they seem initially."

"No . . ."

"It takes time to know anyone."

"Yes, I guess it does."

"Will there be anything else?"

"Gladys, I'm not sure how to ask this. You and my father—"

"Yes, sir?" Her smile is disarming, as if she knows what you need to say. "He was a wonderful man, one I could trust. I miss him very much."

"So do I. You can trust me, too."

"I know that. Thank you, sir."

She returns to making the coffee, then brings you a cup with two packets of sugar and one of Creamora when it is done. Sitting down on the chair beside your desk, both hands folded on her lap, she asks.

"Did you decide?"

You tell her you have, lifting the cup, sipping carefully so as not to scald your lips. Your secretary has always taken her lunches alone. You know why, but today you will ask her to join you and Nips at Etta's near the Pike Place Market.

"Shall I ring that person for you?"

"I think so, it must be eleven in Atlanta by now."

ALEX KOTLOWITZ

WHERE WAS THE VILLAGE?

The stench of urine and rotting garbage is overwhelming, as is the palatable fear that around the next corner lurks a young man with a gun. This is the Ida B. Wells public housing complex on Chicago's South Side, a collection of red brick high-rises that hover over a labyrinthian maze of what might generously be called townhouses. Street gangs so control the complex that at night they roll garbage dumpsters into the streets to slow the traffic; it prevents drive-bys from rival gangs. In some buildings, they won't allow residents in or out at night so that they can deal drugs uninterrupted. It is like most public housing in Chicago: drab, dreary, and desolate. There are no movie theaters, skating rinks, or bowling alleys for the children. There is but one restaurant. And the residents share one grocery store with the thousands of others who inhabit the nearby two-mile State Street corridor of public housing. It is, in short, devoid of the businesses and institutions that define community.

In the early evening hours of October 13, 1994, two boys, aged ten and eleven, dangled five-year-old Eric Morse from a fourteenth-floor window here. Eric wouldn't steal candy for them. As Eric's feet spun furiously in the air, he pleaded with his tormentors to pull him back in. They dropped him to his death.

His killers displayed no remorse. In court the younger of the two, who could barely see the judge above the partition, mouthed obscenities at reporters covering the trial. In February 1996, they became the youngest offenders ever sent to prison in Illinois. And they've come to symbolize the coming of the so-called superpredators, children accused of maiming or killing without a second thought. What is going on?

Both boys had fathers who at one time or another were incarcerated, one for a drug offense, the other for home invasion and stalking. One had a mother who, according to school records, repeatedly missed counseling sessions. The other mother, according to court records, battled a drug addiction. I don't mention this by way of excusing the crime, one so heinous that it makes me shake with anger. Nor do I mention this to state the obvious: In the absence of loving, nurturing, discipline-minded adults, children become lost. Rather, I want to point out that we can debate all we want the justness of meting out long prison sentences, but what about the life to which these children had already been condemned? It seems safe to assume that neither of these children had a stable family life. Yet, we profess homage to the well-worn aphorism that it takes a village to raise a child. Where in the case of these boys—and ultimately Eric Morse—was the village?

Let's take a look at the older of the two boys, who I will call James. He attended the J. R. Doolittle Schools, both the primary and intermediate branches, two buildings that butt up against what the children call the Ida Bs. James earned mediocre grades, mostly Cs, and then in the third grade when his father got arrested his grades plunged. He couldn't sit still in class. He fought with other students. In fourth grade, the school ordered a psychological evaluation, which recommended only tutoring. That same year, he flunked every subject, including gym and music. Nonetheless, the school promoted him. The next year, he missed twenty-three days of school. Because of his continuing low grades, his new school, the intermediate Doolittle branch, made him repeat the fifth grade.

Didn't the schools sense that something was amiss in this child's life? Where were the psychologists and social workers? The primary school, which James attended through fourth grade, can only afford to have one psychologist and one social worker come once a week for its seven hundred children. Where were the truant officers? Three years ago, the financially strapped Chicago Public Schools axed them from its budget.

One afternoon, when James was on his way to pick up his cousin at school, he witnessed a teenaged gang member shoot and kill a rival. James was nine at the time. According to his attorney, Michelle Kaplan, he was standing ten feet from the victim. In most communities, such a bloody incident would have brought quick attention. I'm reminded of the day when in 1988 Laurie Dann, a deranged woman, walked into Winnetka, Illinois's Hubbard Woods Elementary School and shot six children, killing an eight-year-old boy. The community brought in a crisis team of psychologists and social workers to counsel the children as well as their parents and teachers. The governor called for tighter school security. Some politicians demanded tougher gun control legislation.

After this gang shooting, did any adult counsel James? Did any adult tell him they'd do what they could to make sure such an incident didn't happen again? The answer to these questions is "no." Yet, the consequence of witnessing such trauma is clear. Children don't become used to the violence; they find ways, often self-destructive ways, to accommodate it in their lives. A 1995 article in the *Journal of the American Medical Association* concluded that witnessing a stabbing or shooting causes depression, anger, anxiety, and dissociation. It's not at all unusual to find young boys in a community like the Ida Bs with dark circles under their eyes, children who clearly have trouble sleeping. Or to find children unable to sit still in the classroom; such hyperactivity is common among trauma victims. Or children who unsurprisingly deal with conflict in violent ways.

Where were the police in this village? In the six months before Eric's murder, the police arrested James eight times on relatively minor charges ranging from shoplifting to possession of ammunition, presumably bullets. Each time the police released him. After three arrests in one year, the police are supposed to—by their own guidelines—refer the child to juvenile court in the hope that he or she might receive help. That was never done in the case of James.

"This was a child in crisis," Ms. Kaplan said. "Here's an eleven-year-old child who was expressing, in the way that only a child can, that something's wrong here."

For the better part of three decades the city's public housing authority has been most notable by its disregard of, if not total absence from, the lives of children like James. The physical state of Chicago's public housing would depress almost anyone. At Ida B. Wells, naked lightbulbs illuminate the hallways, naked cinderblock lines the walls of residences. (As I write this, the Chicago Housing Authority, now in receivership, has undertaken a renovation of the complex, including the demolition of some buildings.) There are two playgrounds for the nearly 5,000 residents; one of them sits smack in the middle of a parking lot. And perhaps most unsettling for the parents, the homes at Ida B. Wells were painted with lead-based paint that now chipping and flaking has become a hazard to young children. Some children have been found to have high levels of lead, which can lead to developmental difficulties and learning disabilities.

In 1994 the authority did not have the money to renovate apartments as they became vacant, so many dwellings were simply boarded up. Some buildings hosted more vacant than occupied apartments. Moreover, the authority had not installed safety bars on the high-rise windows. The boys who dropped Eric to his death had commandeered such an empty apartment, using it as a clubhouse— and it was through the barless window that they dropped their friend.

Yet the village vigorously ends up debating not how we failed James but, more predictably, what we should do with him: send him to prison or to a residential center, where the emphasis is on rehabilitation? The latter is how we hand out justice in its narrowest sense. But what is just about life for kids at Ida B. Wells? The judge who oversaw this case, Carol Kelly, is tough and has a reputation for siding with the prosecution. And indeed, she chose to send the two boys to a youth prison, though with the stipulation that they receive therapeutic treatment. But when asked what she'd like people to take away from this case, Judge Kelly said: "I wish what would come out of this case is not what these kids did but let's focus on what brought them to this point. What happened to them? What didn't happen to them? What can we do so we don't have other Eric Morses?"

I'm haunted by one image in particular. When the two boys dropped Eric from the window, Eric's eight-year-old brother ran down the fourteen flights as fast as he could. He later testified that he was hoping he could catch Eric. Eric's brother did more than anyone else to try to save his little brother. He and Eric are victims of James and his cohort—and of the village guardians who failed them. James and his ten-year-old partner were not headed for trouble; they were well into it. Yet no adult intervened.

These boys come from a neighborhood poor in spirit and resources. If we can't help rebuild their community, we'll all end up running furiously down those flights of stairs hoping, praying that we can catch yet one more child dropped by their families and by the institutions presumably there to serve them. It will almost always be too late.

BEVERLY LOWRY

SECRET CEREMONIES OF
LOVE AND DEATH

My friend Karla Faye got married last June, changed her last name from Tucker to Brown. This came as no surprise. She'd been calling herself by her new name for a long time already, months before the actual ceremony took place. In the eyes of God, she'd explained, she and Dana Brown had taken their vows, made their commitment already. The only thing left was, as she said, to put it on paper for man's sake. "Love," she ended her letters, "Karla Faye Brown (SMILE!)."

No matter her legal last name, the Texas Department of Correction will continue to call Karla Faye by her inmate identification number, 777, from now until . . . I do what I can to skip over some possibilities. Until whatever happens regarding her case. When the Houston *Chronicle* got wind of the wedding, its page-one story was headlined, "New Bride Can't Leave Death Row." The first sentence of the story began, "Pickax murderer Karla Faye Tucker . . . has married."

I grew up in a time of absolutes. Purity, goodness, evil. Those days, the righteous, honorable, and true soul suited up to do battle against the enemies of God and America (weren't they the same?) and we all knew who they were. The belief in purity makes for sanctimoniousness and—worse—a kind of cynicism that denies people second and third chances. Certainty becomes a razor-toothed trap, which clamps hard down on the heart and spirit. I was raised Christian but not a serious one. Presbyterians went to church, certainly, but church never got in the way of how you lived or what you ate. When I was sixteen, I even went to a religious camp in the Rockies, where I declared myself saved and—standing before a roomful of converts and weeping friends—dedicated my life to Jesus. My conversion also did not seriously change my life. When camp was over, I reverted to former desires: to be a cheerleader and a member of the Sub-Deb Cotillion Club.

Things happen, Compassion softens certainty. Harsh concepts come clean. The curious heart opens, and we begin to understand just how complex good is and how twisted happiness can be. Life does this and that; we end up in situations we once would have thought of as dead-end and hopeless. And yet, once we stop beating our heads against stony facts and come to a point when we can consider the options, we can still manage, not just to convince ourselves, but actually to know and to believe, "This is good. I am content." Considering the issue of hope, Karla Faye quotes Scripture, Romans 4:18, in which Paul, speaking of Abraham, says, "Who, contrary to hope, in hope believed."

Karla Faye didn't personally attend her wedding and, by her request, neither did any of her family or friends. Newspapers didn't get wind of the nuptials until the next day. Karla seriously did not want to get married by proxy; she wanted to stand with Dana Brown hand in hand, so that they could say their vows together. She thought maybe she'd be on bench warrant in Houston for a court date and they could have the service then, or even that a judge might sympathize and give her permission to leave prison for her wedding; but it didn't happen, and in the end proxy was her only choice. But the groom was there, a minister performed the ceremony, and afterwards, Karla Faye's new husband drove to the prison in his car with "Just Married" painted all over it and balloons trailing from the back bumper, so that Karla Faye could see it from the window in her cell as he made the turn to the parking lot by the gates to the visiting room. With the other women on death row, the bride had been having her own ceremony and celebration, with cake and small presents.

The wedding took place on a Saturday, so that Karla Faye and Dana could eat together during their weekly visit, Saturday being the only day TDC allows death-row inmates to have a meal with visitors. But TDC didn't cook that particular night, and so they drank Cokes together and didn't care at all about the food. "The first thing we did," Dana says, "was fall on our knees and pray." He was in his wedding suit, she in prison-issue whites, and the newly-weds had their wedding night visit sitting in hard folding chairs with a shield of Plexiglas between them. They pretended to touch one another through the Plexiglas; they held up their hands in a thumb and forefinger salute, their hand signal for love; they crossed their arms over their chests and rocked back and forth and hugged their own shoulders as a substitute for holding one another; they prayed together for a long, long time. "Mush through the mesh," they call what happens when they are together.

And after their visit, when Dana's two hours were up, Karla went back to her quarters, with the five other women on Texas's death row, where she was locked up in her cell for the night, and after eating dinner with friends, Dana Brown went home to the condominium he has bought, where he and Karla hope, in time, to have a life together. "I am," Karla reported to me in a letter, "definitely the blushing bride, feeling every bit the in-love young married woman."

I met Karla Faye in 1986, two years after the death of my son Peter, who at eighteen had been killed in a hit-and-run occurrence I still refuse to call an accident. Death was on my mind all the time in those years. I felt alone with death, wed to it, in its thrall. I'd done what I could to mend my heart: psychotherapy, psychics, a fortune-teller with candles and cards. Family and friends provided me with soft pillows of love and compassion. And I had, in fact, been able to go on with my life. I seemed better and was, but barely. Crookedly creeping along. Then I saw a newspaper story about Karla Faye, the changes she'd experienced in prison, her newfound religion, the happiness she'd discovered on death row. There was a color picture: Karla Faye with a chipped tooth, chin cupped in one hand, hair curled around her face, those dark soft eyes taking the camera straight on. A pretty young woman in prison whites, she looked sweet and soulful and—I could think of no other word to describe what I saw—*good*. And yet at her trial she had been described by her own lawyer as evil incarnate. I didn't get it. Captivated by what I saw—she was so alive—I wrote and went to see her.

Women don't so much create a friendship as discover it. When I walked into the visiting room and found Karla Faye sitting on her side of the Plexiglas saying "Howdy" and broadly beckoning me over to where she was, I knew I would not easily walk away from whatever this relationship turned out to be. And I sat in the metal folding chair and I asked her questions, and she told me everything. The murders. Her life. Her mother. Sex, drugs. I listened, listened. Then I told her about Peter and how he died, and, to make the point that she *deserved* to be where she was, she asked an amazing question: "Now what if they found the person who hit Peter and they put him on trial and he said, 'But I'm sorry now. I'm different. I've changed.' How would you feel?"

We challenge each other's easy assumptions. When she looked at me—dead-on, not flinching—with the same soft sweetness I saw in the newspaper photo, I had to admit, I didn't know. "See?" she said.

At that time she'd been on death row for two years, in prison for three. I'd lived in Houston when her trial took place. I remembered it well: the double murders, the horrible weapon of death, the reported claims of the defendant—my friend, who was twenty-three at the time—to have felt sexually gratified by what she'd done that horrible night, an erotic peak with every stroke. That braggy statement did Karla in, in the eyes of her jury, and more than likely put her on death row. When I asked her about it, she winced. Of course it wasn't true. She only said it because of who she said it *to,* and how badly she wanted to be one of them—in her druggy sped-up state of mind and tomboy heart wanting to be a tough guy, running with bikers, not wanting to be girly and hesitant, needing instead to be bold, ballsy, a lover of violence and trouble. It was the kind of murder death-penalty advocates use as a test case to prove their point:

that there are people who are, oh very unlike the rest of us, people who are born bad. Monstrous, these others, they walk among us, dead to hope and unredeemable, unworthy to enjoy access to the constitutional rights the rest of us hold dear. Or even, to live.

And there she sat, a warm, loving, thinking young woman. She had told about the murders in the penalty phase of her trial, told of her life: the marijuana at eight, heroin at ten. She even testified against the man who gave her lessons in killing, the thirty-five-year-old boyfriend who was with her the night of the murders. I listened to her story and believed. Trusted her. And I thought I could perhaps speak for her, even speak *as* her, and if I did I might understand a little more about the complexities of good and evil and hope and cynicism. And in doing so, I might lift our spirits—hers and mine and even other people's—marginally higher.

Randomness is hard to take. The nighttime chop, where? Here, there? Out of the blue. Having nothing to do with fault, blame or deserving. Fate will do, in a pinch. At the time I met Karla, I was still looking for a narrative that would make my life, my son's death, make sense. Time to time, I still look for it. Peter's death—to state the obvious—changed my life. Hearing Karla's story—hours and hours sitting across from one another in the TDC visiting room, freezing in the ice-cold Texas air-conditioning, doing yoga poses for one another, drinking soft drinks from a machine, separated always by the cloudy Plexiglas—altered that change. There we sat, both of us with death on our minds, swapping stories. I went to see her once a week for about a year. We could not touch—have never—or exchange any items in person. A guard watched over our every move. And so she sent me photographs of herself and her family, wrote long letters describing her childhood, let me in on private information. Some secrets I keep hidden yet. I still go to see her, though not as often now.

People say (but everybody loves Karla now) she is a new person, isn't she? This girl you go to see, she surely is not the Karla Faye who helped commit murder, is she? We long for certainty, the defined personality, the fixed, known thing; childlike, we still believe in it.

The Karla Faye I visit is not new but the Karla who always was, who might have been, the true Karla Faye who walked among us and did wrong but was always herself the warm, thinking, good young woman I know, who only emerged in prison, minus drugs and bikers and the need to be a tough guy. This is who she will be from now on. Karla Faye gave me not only consolation but a broader sense of the scope of human possibility. Once you know how complex action and motivation and a whole long life can be, you adjust your assumptions, reconsider concepts, enlarge whatever notion you once had of the limits of what might be. Cynicism is tried, tested, and hung up like meat on a hook, to be explored, dissected, maybe even discarded.

Hold up the scales. Hope on one end, cynicism on the other. We've heard it all before. "Sure she's a Christian," we say. On death row, wouldn't you be?

Soften. Listen. Give her a chance. I would come home from the prison and lie in bed and at some dark late hour begin to doubt. Was I being gulled? No. Like falling in love, sometimes you simply *know.* Be still. Trust your heart. If she is not truthful and trustworthy— I knew this—nobody ever was.

A couple of months before Karla got married, I met her new husband. Dana Brown is a handsome, easygoing prison minister who travels the world visiting prisons, singing songs with inmates and reading Scripture to them, trying to bring people hope, and to Jesus. I sat in the visiting room with him—us on the free side of the Plexiglas, Karla on the other—and watching them, I thought of all the variations of love I'd known of, all the people who have maintained love through the most god-awful, unimaginable circumstances, and, put in that context, the limitations imposed on the love of these two young people didn't seem that outrageous to me. "People think I'm crazy," Dana shrugged. "That's okay. They don't think I can touch Karla but I do. We touch spirits all the time, visibly, in that room and even when we're not together. I wouldn't change anything." They praised Jesus a lot that day and said how they'd been married in the eyes of the Lord for a long time. They had fasted for a month, prayed hard, waited. Once they declared

their love for one another, Dana had to give up the privilege of actually going into the death row unit where Karla lives, to lead the
women there in prayer and song. He became an ordinary visitor,
like me, permanently stuck on the other side of the Plexiglas.

She is, my friend Karla Faye, the least cynical person I know. As
for the death penalty, well—it shames us all. In the end, read
enough cases and the truth becomes clear: Who dies by needle or
electric current, administered by the state—us—is arbitrary and
has more to do with circumstance—economics and race—than the
crime committed. Like hit-and-run, it falls on the unlucky ones
whose roll of the dice comes up short. No woman has been executed
in Texas since 1896, when Chipita Rodriguez was hung from a
hackberry tree for stealing a horse. Now that women run marathons
and countries, is it time to punish them equally as well? To bring
the statistics up to date with the times? Poke women's arms the
same as men's, fill their veins with poison, steal their breath and
heartbeat?

One night it either happens. Or it doesn't. The wind turns;
there's a new, breeze-born scent in the air, freshly elected governor,
the politics of the moment. One night the deal comes down. Somebody says, Go. Stop. Or, Wait.

Sadness, once rooted in the heart, never dies. Appalling, the
things that happen, the boy on the highway alone, dying, unat-
tended. Two people murdered in their beds, the young woman sentenced to die. Karla sends me jokes, pretty cards, pictures cut from
magazines, a page full of wildly colored women's cowboy boots:
Which ones do I like? She describes the house Dana Brown has
bought for them and tells me again and again how happy she is.
"My spirit," she says, "soars." Sometimes I think about the possibility of her execution, then I don't. I stuff the possibility back in some
lost drawer of the mind where we jam the unthinkable.

When I first met Karla, there were four women on death row;
now there are six. In letters, she tells me about their legal appeals,
their life together. I send her postcards from wherever I go and tell
her stories about places, people, my dog. She is not afraid to die, but
oh, I don't want her to. Sometimes, working out at the gym, music

pounding in black foam buttons in my ears, I hear an upbeat rock song that reminds me of Karla Faye and I imagine that she is with me, and we are laughing and dancing together, twirling in soft skirts to the beat, alive and happy. And I stop working out and stand there and see myself in some big mirror with a dopey smile on my face.

In the end, I can't save Karla Faye, and neither can Dana Brown. The random nighttime chop hits where it will. It's Karla who, *contrary to hope . . .*

More than either of us and whatever happens, *in hope believes.*

RUNAWAY JURORS:
RACE VERSUS THE EVIDENCE

If one really wishes to know how justice is administered in a country, one does not question the policemen, the lawyers, the judges, or the protected members of the middle class. One goes to the unprotected—those, precisely, who need the law's protection most!—and listens to their testimony.

JAMES BALDWIN, *NO NAME IN THE STREET*

Our civilization has decided . . . that determining the guilt or innocence of men is a thing too important to be trusted to trained men. . . . When it wants a library catalogued, or the solar system discovered, or any trifle of that kind, it uses up its specialists. But when it wishes anything done which is really serious, it collects twelve of the ordinary men standing round. The same thing was done, if I remember right, by the Founder of Christianity.

G. K. CHESTERTON, "TWELVE MEN," *TREMENDOUS TRIFLES*

Juries, it is often said, should not take the law into their hands. But, of course, they do. It's their job—or, at least, part of it.

History, customs, and tradition have assigned two jobs to juries. One is to determine guilt or innocence. The other is to decide justice by determining how the law is to be enforced. The first job punishes the guilty. The second protects the innocent.

That second job is tricky. Even experts sometimes forget about it—or try to.

In Alan M. Dershowitz's book about the O. J. Simpson trial, *Reasonable Doubts,* he recalls asking a friend who also happened to be a judge whether he thought a jury should acquit a drug dealer because police lied to them, even though the jury knew the dealer was guilty: "He [the judge] quickly said no. I then asked him what he would do as a judge if he concluded that the police had planted evidence against a convicted defendant he believed guilty. 'I'd throw the conviction out,' he said. 'Even if you knew the defendant was guilty?' I pressed him. 'Absolutely,' he replied. I asked him what the difference was. He responded: 'I'm a judge. It's my job to make sure the system isn't polluted by evidence tampering.'"[1]

Fair enough. But jurors also think it is their job to make sure the judicial system is working right. Take, for example, the Simpson trial. Interviews with Simpson trial jurors reveal at least some of them thought Simpson probably was guilty. So did I. But when the system is working the way it is supposed to, "probably" is not enough. Guilt is supposed to be determined "beyond a reasonable doubt." The enduring good sense of the presumption of innocence was best stated by Sir William Blackstone: "It is better that ten guilty persons escape than that one innocent suffer."[2] If that system did not work the same for blacks as for whites, we would have justifiable reason for the sort of uprising that followed the acquittal of police who beat Rodney King.

Johnnie Cochran may actually have muddied the waters when he told jurors to acquit Simpson to "send a message" to police. In interviews jurors, three of whom were not black, have said it was not race but the government's failure to prove its case that led to the acquittal. This jury wanted to send a message, not only to police but to the society at large that the presumption of innocence still counts for something.

We don't question this presumption of innocence when it is meted out to a wealthy white man, like William Kennedy Smith, John de Lorean, or Klaus von Bulow. Quite the contrary, as one

1. Alan M. Dershowitz, *Reasonable Doubts: The O. J. Simpson Case and the Criminal Justice System* (New York: Simon and Schuster, 1996), 96.
2. *Commentaries on the Laws of England* (1765–1769), vol. 4, ch. 27.

Howard student put it, it was downright refreshing to see a black man who had become wealthy enough to afford rich white man's justice.

That's not the sort of act that makes you popular when it leads you to make an unpopular decision. Much of the media commentary after the Simpson trial slammed the "black-controlled jury" for being too emotional and refusing to listen to the facts. Take, for example, this angry postverdict assessment by columnist George Will (My emphasis added): "There was condescension, *colored by racism,* in some of the assumptions that the jurors would be incompetent jurors and bad citizens—that they would be putty in the hands of defense attorneys harping on race, that they would be intellectually incapable of following an evidentiary argument, or, worse, they would lack the civic conscience to do so. But *those assumptions seem partially validated* by the jury's refusal even to deliberate."[3]

Never mind, for the moment, that the jury did deliberate for more than three hours. Never mind as well that it included three nonblacks. Let us, for the moment, consider only the proposition that those admittedly racist assumptions seem "partially validated." Why, I ask, is it so easy for distinguished commentators like Will to view this case through the prism of racial bias against black jurors? "It is interesting to contrast Will's easy willingness to assume that the Simpson jury's verdict was based on racial factors with his adamant unwillingness to believe that death penalty verdicts imposed by predominantly white jurors are based on racial factors," notes Dershowitz, who was a member of the Simpson defense team.[4]

Indeed, Will railed in 1987 against those who concluded on the basis of extensive statistics that Georgia juries are four times more likely to impose the death penalty on blacks who kill whites than on whites who kill blacks. He called the data a "statistical discrep-

3. George F. Will, "Circus of the Century," *Washington Post,* 4 October 1995, sec. A25, col. 2.
4. Dershowitz, *Reasonable Doubts,* 134.
5. Ibid.

ancy that coincided with race."[5] He went on to argue that white Georgia juries considered *everything but* race. Yet Will needs no statistics to conclude that the Simpson jury considered *only* race, that the jury was either racist or just stupid. Is that a double standard or what?

No one can read jurors' inner thoughts, but I stand with those who say the Simpson jury did not have to nullify the evidence to reach the conclusion it reached. It only had to interpret the evidence from a perspective that is not an unusual one in black America, the perspective of the oppressed.

Let us presume for the moment that black jurors are no more or less racist or stupid than white jurors. Let us presume instead that black jurors care as much as white jurors about police protection, the burden of proof, the presumption of innocence, and other niceties of the American judicial system. Let us further take for granted in today's America that the life experiences of a randomly selected black juror are *likely* to be significantly different from those of a randomly selected white juror, particularly when it comes to experiences with the criminal justice system. Let us then ask what does *that* have to do with justice in America?

Lawyers almost intuitively know this. Prosecutors are routinely trained to expect black jurors to be harder to persuade than white jurors. Highly paid jury consultants tell their clients the same thing. Yet to say that blacks tend to be more skeptical of police and prosecutors is not the same as saying blacks are soft on crime. The incarceration of young black males has reached record proportions, taking up almost half of the national jail population, even though blacks are only 10 percent of the general population. The vast majority were put there by black jurors.

The most distressing aspect of the Simpson verdict may have been its implication of racial payback, a shot fired in a low-level racial war, the nightmare vision of black bigots doing to whites what whites traditionally have done to blacks. Yet there is evidence that many black jurors may be letting guilty defendants go free, not out of a sense of payback but out of a sense of justice overlooked by traditional processes.

"The life of the law has not been logic: It has been experience," wrote Oliver Wendell Holmes Jr.[6] I would argue that racial experience, not racial prejudice, weighs most profoundly on the credence black jurors give to the prosecution in cases like this one. Prosecutor Marcia Clark's closing argument defied common sense when she conceded that her star witness, Mark Fuhrman, was a rabid racist—that he especially hated interracial couples, that he sometimes planted evidence and then lied about it under oath—and then asked the jury to shrug all of that off, as if it had nothing at all to do with the O. J. Simpson case.

No, the O. J. jury did not have to negate, neutralize, or counteract the evidence. It only had to interpret it in light of their own common sense. Experience may not always be the best teacher, but its lessons are the most enduring. As black comedian Chris Rock would perceptively put it to a theater audience later, "A white jury would have done the same thing . . . [pause] . . . if the defendant had been [Jerry] Seinfeld . . . [pause] . . . and the person who found the [bloody] glove just happened to be from the Nation of Islam!"

Others disagree. "Trials in a free country," fumed syndicated columnist Charles Krauthammer, a lawyer and psychiatrist, after the verdict, "are supposed to be about what happened on the night of the crime, not about what generally happens elsewhere in society. A jury box is not a polling booth or a venue for political demonstration."[7]

That's easy to say when you're a member of an empowered majority. In a democratic society, the majority always wins. But what about those occasions when you are in the majority and the system constructed by the majority for its benefit appears, by all indications, to be rigged against you? Do you not take whatever power you have at hand, including jury power, and use it?

I would submit that jurors are not undermining the system when they bring into the courtroom the perspectives that these different experiences produce. Quite the opposite, these off-the-

6. *The Common Law* (Boston: Little, Brown, 1881).
7. Charles Krauthammer, "The Case of the Manufactured 'Victim,'" *Chicago Tribune*, 9 October 1995, sec. 1, at 15.

street views are introduced into the system when the system of judgment by one's peers is working the way it is supposed to do.

The question raised by the O. J. case and other racially charged criminal cases in recent years is: How much of a role should considerations of race play in that pursuit of justice?

The easy answer would be to say that race should play no role at all. But as long as race plays a major role in the interactions of the larger American society, it would be naive, even dangerous, to presume it could play no role in court.

Many African Americans, faced with the twin crises of high crime rates and high incarceration rates, are asking whether there might be a better way to deal with both. One of them is Professor Paul Butler of George Washington University Law School. One way to do it, he says, is jury nullification, a jury's power to neutralize laws it believes to be unjust, even when it frees the guilty.

He does not think it happened in the Simpson case, nor does he think it should have. But, for nonviolent petty crimes, Butler calls on black jurors to free black criminals, even if they are guilty. "I now believe that, for pragmatic and political reasons, the black community is better off when some non-violent lawbreakers remain in the community rather than go to prison," he writes.

His views, expressed in a *Yale Law Review* article published almost simultaneously with the Simpson verdict, raised national controversy, including a *60 Minutes* interview by a wincing, highly skeptical Mike Wallace. But he is not your garden-variety bomb thrower. He is a Harvard and Yale trained former federal prosecutor for the District of Columbia. It was only after sending a seemingly endless procession of young black males to jail that he decided the system was no longer serving black community needs. In fact, he quotes a right-winger like former Los Angeles Police Commissioner Daryl Gates in saying that we are trying to use the criminal justice system to solve too many of society's problems that should be solved some other way.

If Congress, the White House, and state governments are too conservative and isolated to care about black community problems or perspectives, Butler posits, it is incumbent on black folk to take matters into their own hands: They should free young, nonviolent, and redeemable suspects, even if they are guilty, and work to rehabilitate them in the community.

"Whether I hold these views or not, it isn't important," he says. "Black jurors already are nullifying what they see as essentially victimless crimes." Like many other prosecutors, Butler was instructed to expect black juries to be more skeptical than whites of the police and prosecutors. He recalls at least a couple of cases he prosecuted that left him convinced the predominately black juries ignored the evidence out of reluctance to send yet another young black male to jail for a relatively minor, first-time offense.

"They know what they're doing," Butler tells me over lunch in downtown Washington, near the White House. "They know that when a nineteen-year-old black male comes out of prison, he's not going to move to Georgetown [an affluent D.C. neighborhood]. He's going right back to the community. Black jurors know this. It is a self-interested decision on their part. Black jurors already are deciding not to send more young black men to jail."

"Police say they disproportionately enforce drug laws in black communities because the community wants it. Well, do they? Mike Wallace asked me [during the *60 Minutes* interview], what message is the black community going to receive from my call to let nonviolent offenders go free? Well, what's the message they are getting now?"

———

Un-American? Hardly. Jury nullification is deeply rooted in American legal history. Prosecutors would rather jurors not even know about it; because the Double Jeopardy Clause of the Fifth Amendment prevents prosecutors from appealing an acquittal, regardless of the jury's reasons for it, prosecutors would rather see juries vote on the naked facts in such cases not the merits of the law—or their consciences.

Yet as Butler's paper details, the prerogative of juries to check tyranny by judging the law as well as the facts was firmly established in colonial times. In the landmark *Bushell's Case* in 1670, an appeals court refused to uphold the punishment of a jury that acquitted two Quakers, an unpopular minority group, who had been charged with unlawful assembly and disturbance of the peace. Another colonial jury established American freedom of the press in voting to acquit New York publisher John Peter Zenger of seditious libel for publishing statements critical of the British colonial rule. After the founding of the United States, several northern juries nullified the guilt of abolitionists who helped free black slaves, neutralizing laws that viewed escaped slaves as stolen property.

But American courts began to harden their hearts against jury nullification by the late nineteenth century as some state decisions that allowed the practice were overruled. In the 1895 case of *Sparf v. United States,* the Supreme Court upheld a judge who refused to allow two men on trial for murder to instruct the jury that it could convict them of manslaughter, a lesser offense. Quite the opposite, the judge instructed the jurors that any acquittal or conviction of any crime less than murder would be a violation of their legal oath and duties. In essence, the high court ruled that jurors have the power to nullify, but no right to be informed of this power.

Sparf has been largely upheld since then, although some courts have been less critical than others. The District of Columbia Circuit softened its impact in *United States v. Dougherty* (1972), saying that the ability of juries to nullify was widely recognized as "a necessary counter to case-hardened judges and arbitrary prosecutors." Still, the court noted, this necessity did not establish "as an imperative" that a jury be informed by the judge of its power to nullify. Specifically, "what makes for health as an occasional medicine would be disastrous as a daily diet."

Yet it is just the sort of diet prescribed by civil rights dissidents, antiwar protesters, and other activists since the 1950s who asked juries to forgive their acts of civil disobedience against laws and policies they saw as unjust. In that spirit, Professor Butler prescribes the same diet for the imbalances against black Americans he detects in the criminal justice system. For example, when white conservative legislators pass laws that disproportionately throw young black criminals in jail while cutting back on antipoverty programs that attack the root causes of crime, it constitutes to Butler what Lani Guinier and, earlier, James Madison called "the tyranny of the majority." It is incumbent on black Americans to respond with any power they have, Butler says, including the power to serve on juries and nullify what they see as unjust prosecutions.

"Jury nullification is not democratic," he says. "That's why I like it. It's a tool for minorities to use the check the tyranny of the majority."

Butler breaks into a wry smile. "It's using the master's tools to dismantle the master's house. [The late black feminist poet] Audre Lorde said you couldn't use the master's tools to destroy the master's house. Well, yes, you can. Jury nullification is one way to do it."

———

One is hard-pressed to find a juror who will admit to nullifying because of race, but evidence is beginning to mount. One of the more blatant examples involved the case against Darryl Smith, a black drug dealer in Washington, D.C., who tortured eighteen-year-old Willie Wilson, also black, to death as he begged for mercy in front of witnesses. Despite massive evidence presented in his 1990 murder trial, an all-black local jury acquitted Smith. According to other jurors, forewoman Valerie Blackmon argued that the "criminal justice system is stacked against blacks" and refused to convict because "she didn't want to send any more young black men to jail." Three weeks after Smith was let off, D.C. Superior Court received a letter claiming to be from an anonymous juror who expressed regret over the verdict.

Some prosecutors say the racial defense is appearing more often and being heard more often, particularly in areas where distrust of police is high. One Atlanta-area assistant district attorney was quoted in *The American Enterprise* magazine[8] as estimating that one-fourth of all criminal cases that end in acquittal may involve some form of racial nullification. The magazine goes on to quote Bureau

8.   "When Race Trumps Truth in Court," *American Enterprise,* January/February 1996.

of Justice statistics that show rates of felony prosecution and conviction are slightly lower for blacks than whites in the nation's seventy-five largest counties. Nationwide the felony acquittal rate for
defendants of all races is only 17 percent, but in the Bronx, where
more than eight out of ten jurors is either black or Hispanic, 48 percent of all black felony defendants are acquitted. Criminologist
John DiIulio went so far as to say that "blacks are being substan-
tially and systematically under-prosecuted today, not only in cases
of black-on-white crime, but also in cases of black-on-black."

Yet, the most eloquent defense of the Simpson jury may have
come from a most unlikely source, the very conservative, in a free-
market libertarian tradition, editorial page of the *Wall Street Journal*. "We can't know whether Mark Fuhrman's racist tapes tipped
the case against the prosecution," it said. "But it's clear that the 12
women and men of the Simpson jury clearly do not trust the law enforcement institutions of Los Angeles. That may be galling to those
who believe that any disinterested assessment of the prosecution's
case against O. J. Simpson was overwhelming. But all who are mad-
dened by this verdict would do well to make their own disinterested
assessment of the credibility of our legal system."[9]

The editorial was appalled that "the most criminally besieged
among us mistrust the people whose job is to protect them from the
criminals."[10] But it also went on to remind us that blacks are not
the only Americans who feel the judicial system is turning on them.
Members of Congress were having second thoughts about giving
more antiterrorism power to the FBI and other agencies in light of
the Branch Davidian siege at Waco and the shootout with the
Weaver family at Ruby Ridge. Small businesspeople felt oppressed
by a runaway tort liability system. Large businesspeople felt oppressed by runaway environmental cases. The *Wall Street Journal's*
own pages had reported how "wild prosecutions based on extreme
child-abuse theories have resurrected the Salem witch trials in a surprising number of American communities."[11]

9.   "The Jury's Right," *Wall Street Journal,* 4 October 1995, sec. A14, col. 1.
10. Ibid.
11. Ibid.

"Whether one is of the political right or left, what must be admitted is that what we have here in total is an astounding level of public cynicism about the law and law enforcement," the editorial concluded. "For all their notoriety, the men and women of that Los Angeles jury are just a small corner of the American criminal justice system. But on Tuesday their verdict offered us a large message about that system. They don't trust it. Neither do a lot of other people. We better find out why."[12]

And fast. Butler is right when he says jury nullification already is happening, whether he approves or not. And his critics are right to say it leads inexorably toward anarchy. Despite Paul Butler's caveat that skeptical jurors should let only "nonviolent" offenders go, some very violent offenders appear to be receiving the benefits of their doubts, freeing them to return to the streets and commit more mischief and mayhem. As much as I agree with his vision of a black community embracing its own and fulfilling the nurturing rehabilitative roles the larger society has abdicated, I also have my doubts that the low-income neighborhoods from which most of them come and to which most will return have the resources to complete the task.

Former U.S. Attorney Joseph DiGenova, Butler's former boss in the prosecutor's office, argues that advocates of jury nullification on racial grounds are "pushing anarchy." If so, it is up to the rest of us who live in the larger, more affluent society to hear the marching sound of jurisprudential anarchy on the rise. Justice is not supposed to mean "just us," as the old and bitter black wisecrack says. It is supposed to mean the quality of being just and fair, the principle of moral rightness and equity. We need to listen to what juries are trying to tell us when they take it into their own hands.

12. Ibid.

SARAH PETTIT

JUSTIFY OUR LOVE

*S*ometimes *there are things you have words for before you have the means to understand them. I recall my junior year in high school, when my classmates readied for the prom and lost their virginity in the gym after hours or in the rooms of our boarding school, and I wandered the woods of New Hampshire looking for a place of belonging. No longer part of a social whirl I never felt connected to and not yet at a place of self-acceptance, I looked to novels and poetry for answers and wondered when and how I had become separate.*

One spring afternoon, the writer James Baldin came to visit. Dressed in a natty white linen suit and accompanied by an efficient male secretary, the aging expatriate gave several lectures and readings, the last one in the grand hall of the school's library. As he paused for a period of questions and answers, I felt myself rising from my seat in the back, speaking before I even knew what issued from my mouth. I can scarcely recall what I said, but I must have been the consumate picture of halting yet questing lesbian sexuality. Mr. Baldwin, recognizing a fellow traveler, smiled kindly and spoke yet more carefully. Without giving too much or drawing attention to my confusion, he suggested everything would be all right, that I should trust time, that I was not alone. And in that minute I glimpsed, if only for a minute, a whole world beyond me, where a language had already been formed for my existence.

JUST US

There's an old Richard Pryor joke that goes something like, "The funny thing about justice is that once you get inside, you realize it's just us." The "inside" Pryor is talking about of course, is, prison, and his epiphany that it's "just us," is the realization that white America's vaunted sense of fair play is but an illusion for those lucky enough to be on the "outside."

While compare and contrast games amid American minority groups are inevitable and legion in the discourse of oppression, they serve only to pit one hard history against another in a sloppy, dissatisying way. I can't count the times I have heard gay leaders make futile pitches like, "If this had happened to a black group, victim, fill-in-blank, there would be outrage from all quarters." The sad fact is that bad things happen to the disempowered all the time (witness the slayings of a lesbian couple in Oregon or of a pair of campers in the Shenandoah Valley or of two men outside a bar in Texas), and there is never enough outrage to quell out anger and sense of injustice (witness the epidemic of church burnings in the South).

I find Pryor's joke useful for another reason: It not only sends up the "inside" quality of being a criminalized minority in America, but it reminds us about the "outside" too. The "outside" here is life beyond prison bars, beyond miscarriages of the law—it's life as blind as justice herself. But the quality of life here, as everywhere, varies, and to be "outside" is for some of us a more complicated matter than simply being free. It can mean we haven't been caught yet.

Shortly after my encounter with Mr. Baldwin, I went to visit my lesbian aunt in Texas. My parents, either through total blindness or some enlightened sense that I needed mentoring, sent me to stay with her one hot August in Houston. That same summer, my best friend was vacationing with her family in the Gulf town of Kemah, a couple hours drive outside of the city. I was to split my time, two weeks in the gay neighborhood of Montrose and two weeks in an elite, George Bush country yachting community, a great divide whose differences I would not understand fully until years later.

The first two weeks I stayed at my aunt's garage garret, smoking Pall Malls, drinking Tecate beer, and struggling with my awkward instinctual sense that my relative and I shared more than a love of Bonnie Raitt.

Rebecca, then in her early thirties, was that blessed combination of implicitly loving and never too pushy, which meant that we never spoke of anything overtly and yet there were no major secrets. If she knew I was battling with my emerging lesbian feelings she never said so. And yet she allowed me to see, feel, and experience firsthand what a gay life might be.

Being with Rebecca, I never felt different—at least not until the day my friend and her aunt came to pick me up. They came to collect me in the late afternoon, knocking at Rebecca's door and hovering briefly in the entryway. All of a sudden, the cool okre-colored rooms of my aunt's garret, her cats, and her collection of art were all under scrutiny, not appreciated for the modern hideaway I saw them as.

As I collected my bags, my friend's aunt made short conversation with mine, and we then bid a hasty farewell. To this day, I will never forget the odd discomfort around my departure, how walking down the drive with my two new travelling companions, I felt angry and separate. I didn't know what had happened, except that it was something I understood was only the beginning and not an end.

DON'T ASK, DON'T TELL

Unlike the clear, shameful institutional bias that allows countless young black men to have spent time entangled in the American justice system, American gay and lesbians enter the courts through a membrane other than skin. Yes, the *Bowers v. Hardwick* ruling from the Supreme Court does make it illegal for adults in eighteen states of the Union to engage in private consensual relations in their home, and yes, there are no protections in housing and employment from discrimination in a great many states and cities, but the issue of homosexuality is less starkly one of judge and jury (the Court, thankfully, did not find it legal for the state of Colorado to bar discrimination statutes against gay men and lesbians).

Bias cuts on an altogether different angle for a minority group that is scarcely identifiable. At this late stage of the twentieth century, when everything has become measurable and quantifiable, we are not even sure how many gay Americans exist, the 10 percent figure having long been discredited and more recent studies than

Kinsey's having been plagued by blindspots, not least of which that their subjects have all been male.

The sad fact is that most Americans really don't want to know how many of their sisters, daughters, cousins, and colleagues are gay. To be gay and on the "outside" is less to be denied protections and freedom than it is simply to not count—unanimity and sameness are the law until someone is proven different.

Hence gay men and lesbians' need to "come out" and set themselves apart, for to remain silent means to be assumed heterosexual. Ironically, this coming out process has been put through its own judgment process and found wanting. The closet is preferred; complete silence is the ideal. To declare that you are gay or lesbian is seen as an aggressive act, the kind of public flaunting or foisting we hear so much about every year when gay pride parades wend through our cities.

And so while the police may not as readily pull over an eighteen-year-old gay man as they would a black man and assume he has stolen the car he is driving just because he looks gay, they may try to entrap him, as they do on our interstates and in our parks, to solicit sex. Or they may, as they do in the armed forces, just try to get him, or his female coworker, to admit that they are gay or lesbian, grounds enough for dismissal regardless of job performance.

Indeed, the "don't ask, don't tell" policy adopted by the armed forces that allows such discrimination to be enshrined in practice by one of the largest employers in the country is not, as some would have it, an aberration of an antiquated institution but rather a surface sign of attitudes that go deep into the culture at large. Americans prefer not to ask and not be told about homosexuality at all levels—at work, at home, and in public life. But in the military, as elsewhere, there are still ways of being found "out," and when this happens, the consequences can be dire.

Where I come from, "family values" often have less homey applications than their soundbite friendliness implies. Like the military's patter on "unit cohesion" when discussing gay service members, the language of the family is highly politicized and used to cover a host of unsavory, unfamilial acts.

I think of a pal, kicked out of his suburban home at seventeen to live on city streets and at neighbors' houses. Despite a drug problem and a lot of depression, he managed to graduate and win admission to the prestigious college where his father taught, an irony his parents never acknowledged.

I remember another novelist friend, turned out at a similar age to sleep in the boiler room of her high school, wash in its bathrooms, and wander the streets when that small refuge became dangerous. When later as an adult she fought her way to the top of her profession, her parents, who are psychotherapists, remarked only that it was strange that "lesbian pornography" was being reviewed by the New York Times.

I can't forget my friend who came from dirt-poor Cajun roots, made his way to the city, and finally, in his late thirties, achieved the kind of success that few critics attain: He had a book contract, money in the bank, and freedom from waitering jobs for the first time in his life. His parents, Charismatic Christians, had never dealt well with him being gay. When he came down with full-blown AIDS, they were absent but for a phone call or two. Not part of his round-the-clock care team or present at his death, they made a brief final-hour visit, bringing crosses and the bewildered faces of parents who no longer even recognized their son.

THE DEFENSE OF MARRIAGE ACT

Justice is not only elusive, but its path often leads to the least likely places. It is fitting then that the movement for gay marriage, begun in the 1970s, should find its home in the Pacific realm of Hawaii and that the tsunami of social and political issues it raises are now washing up on mainland shores.

The first state to ratify the Equal Rights Amendment in 1970, Hawaii is a Democratic stronghold that rarely countenances right-wing insurgency. When in an act of outsider militancy, Jerry Falwell launched a 1981 campaign to "save the fiftieth state," Hawaiians not only sent Jerry Falwell and his not so Moral Majority packing, but they became, a decade later, the fifth state to offer employment protections for gay men and lesbians.

Perhaps even more interesting than this confluence of histories is the fact that the bid for gay marriage has spawned such vociferous and transparent reactions. Whatever was silent in the American collective subconscious about gay men and lesbians by the 1990s has really come tumbling out in the debate over this most sacred of institutions.

As a populace frequently characterized by its public male stereotypes, gay and lesbian Americans have, through the sexual liberations movement of the 1970s and the crisis over public health and AIDS in the 1980s, been demonized for their home-wrecking, morals-flaunting "promiscuity." Lesbians, rarely seen or understood, have simply been incorporated or overlooked in this broad-brushing, and gay men, like men in every public sphere, have come to characterize the true nature of the beast. Under every major law—take the 1986 Supreme Court sodomy law decision—and every major social debate—take the "gays in the military" flap—one need only dig so far to find the trace elements of gay male sexuality and its allegedly disruptive force on society.

How remarkable then that a movement for gay marriage, and all the stabilizing, socializing strictures it is meant to carry, should arouse such aggressive calls to arms. The first such reaction was the Defense of Marriage Act, a bill to safeguard matrimony from same-sex couples, introduced in Washington during an election year and with a president vulnerable on gay issues. At once a wonderfully contradictory and yet shamelessly literal reaction to gay America's efforts to move "inside," it shows how far from steady the course of justice goes: Our culture, so in need of laws against the free-floating menace of gay men and lesbians, must nonetheless also have legislation against their efforts to "civilize" themselves.

I visit a major television station on the eve of gay pride celebrations, a guest on a panel of expert witnesses on our lives. Our interviewer is green, never having conducted an on-air debate, and he seems nervous and short tempered that his first subjects should be so out of the usual prime-time fare. As we mike up and the cameras roll, it becomes clear this man, like many of the Americans he is speaking to, doesn't understand any of the history or legal status of gay men and lesbians. I try to smile and answer politely as he spins out the pervasive and disquieting notion that we could all roll

*along, not pushing things, and be happy, save for our petulant need to push
or flaunt our case. "What is it," he asks brusquely, "that you people want?"*

And so while Richard Pryor's epiphany clearly locks black Americans away inside one kind of justice system, gay Americans spin dizzyingly in a gravity and logic defying orbit at once inside and outside of the culture. We are told we are seeking "special rights,"but we are discouraged from engaging in the pursuit of equal rights. We are told to civilize ourselves, yet are not allowed access to the places in the culture where the codes of that trumpeted civility are forged. We are pulled by the great American myth that all citizens are part of a vast melting pot and then repelled by the abiding American distaste for difference. We are lured by the fiction that all subjects are treated fairly under the law and cast off by a legal apparatus intent on criminalizing our bodies. Trapped somewhere in the cogs of justice, we are plates that don't fit, parts that slip in the machinery just as they engage it.

*On the night of my thirtieth birthday, I stand in a bar surrounded by a
hundred-odd friends from a decade of life in Manhattan. It's a week before
the memorial service of a young colleague and the crowd is dotted with men
and women, many nearly his age, some older. I wonder about those of us fortunate enough to have made it this far. One friend not in attendance is home
pregnant, her lover explaining that the smoke and noise would be too much
this late in her third trimester. I think about their child and the beginning
they are making amid so much loss and sadness, and wonder what we all
tell that child about this era, swirled as it is with so many adult lessons. I
think that we will tell it that we learned something about justice and even
more about making a place in the gaps we find every day through our love
for one another.*

JUSTICE

Initially, I was demoniacally tickled at the notion that I, Ntozake
Shange, a.k.a. Paulette Linda Williams, whose American birth
certificate from an alleged Union state, New Jersey, read "colored"
in 1948, was asked to write a piece about justice. This was truly
laughable, since it is quite clear to me that "justice" as a fact, fan-
tasy, or concept is so removed an actuality in my life, intellectual as
well as visceral, that I thought maybe I should try my hand at a
myth or my first science fiction. But the blues has not always made
me or my people unhappy, you see; this idea is false. The general
ideas roaming American minds—black, white, Asian, Chicano,
Texan, urban, empty of truth whichever they are about who and
what I come from and what is "just" for us—are as scary as the bul-
let holes by Huey Long's assassination in Baton Rouge and as sad as
The Trail of Tears, and I haven't gotten to "the Negro" yet. We are
essentially a generous people, not eager to chasten or exploit. But I
can say right here and now that the absence of a day in honor of the
end of slavery in this country is shameful, which to my mind makes
it unjust—the opposite of justice.

To my mind, justice is inconceivable in an envision of ignorance,
yet the truth of the inescapable essential ties of slave trade to the so-
called Renaissance, the evolution of an industrial workforce, and the
globalization of trade, economics, and politics is a thought "foreign"

to the American mind. The word "manumission" cannot be used in
ordinary conversations, references to The Freedmen's Project are left
hanging in the awkward silence of lack of knowledge the way our
bodies hung from tree limbs for days and nobody saw nothin' to cut
down. Far and away the most painful aspect of this wishful absent-
ing of Africans from "our" own history is the terrible isolation experienced by those of us who are descendants of the Diaspora in the
New World.

———

Only because my father wasn't W. E. B. Du Bois, Paul Robeson, or
Walter White, I assume, he carried a valid American passport, as
did my mother with whom he traveled. I am so lucky, fortunate,
blessed to have seen actual footage (in black and white, no less) of
Haitians, Dominicans, Costa Ricans, Congolese going about their
daily business in modern times, using automobiles, electric radios,
elevators, freeways, books; let's not forget books. I say this without
aplomb because I was laughed at in all but a few of the schools I attended if I so much as suggested that: (1) there were Africans outside the United States who had not ever been owned by anyone, or
(2) if they were property in some contorted system of justice, they
did not necessarily speak English, and (3) they voted and ate in
restaurants, went to libraries and took buses, unlike any of the Negroes (I have no idea what they called us out of my earshot) they
knew—therefore, I was really a silly little ninny to speak of such ab-
surdities as the lives of black folk. Even then, our longing for our
song, our place on the face of this earth, summarily dismissed.

Slavery was such a long time ago.

Why can't I forget about all that and get on with my life? I'd
like to, believe me. But, not unlike other humans who suffer
trauma or brain-washing (a very popular phrase during my childhood), I was raised surrounded by public images of people who
looked like me, who looked and acted like what I was told slaves, at
least the black ones, looked and acted like. Right after the first television sets were available commercially, I was apparently watching
cartoons with my mother, who shut the thing off. "Why, Mom?

Why?" I cried. The answer made no sense to me then. She said something I don't remember, but I instinctively recall as uncontestable. Mother, Eloise Williams, wrote the network that the cartoon with Epaminondous chasing himself around a tree till he caught up with his own stereotypical Ubangi lips, which turned into pancakes that he smacked as black and happy as poor Uncle Tom never knew, was inappropriate for modern America. Yet, Buckwheat and The Little Rascals regularly performed impromptu minstrel shows black face and all. "The Blues Singer" featuring Eddie Cantor, of course, introduced me to the history of Yiddish Theatre, the plight of southern Europeans on the Lower East Side, and the absolute disdain held for what I came from by everyone in the world, I imagined. Everybody knew, even I, that Paul Henreid, Tyrone Power, Errol Flynn, and James Cagney had saved the world over and over in moving black and white frames from fascism and hatred of differences. It was very clear to me that whoever I was and wherever I came from had an extremely tenuous relationship to other living things, besides cotton, cane, sleeping cars, shoe shine stands, bozo's unshined shoes, gorillas on the Empire State Building, heads of unknown colored people decorating Carolinian roads for pleasure, for a laugh, for terror ? I don't know.

I'm beginning to feel like the homeless man who haunts and taunts residents of the Upper West Side. I am lost in the confoundment of what it is I'm supposed to be, do, say, respect, cherish. I want to make some noise and bash some heads. Run the Boers into the sea. Take all the Ashante art out the basement of the British Museum, out the basement of the Met for that matter. When I talk about what I imagine to be just, I sound like a crazy wild niggah roaming the streets and dangerous to American "civilization" (I have heard it called that, "civilization"). Anyway, I'm a doctor's daughter who was presented to "society" at the Waldorf, who graduated from a Seven Sister College, and I'm just as lacking in understanding American justice as Bessie Smith on her way to a hospital what took colored, or Emmett Till's mother. I'm not even close to approaching the gall and ungracious sadism demonstrated when white folks ask, "Well, what's it like to be, uh, 'black in America'?"

But it was all so long ago. The whole country going wild cause a niggah allegedly kill a white woman. Entire news editorials stunned by the burning of black churches, the mutating of young black men's souls and bodies on the sidewalks with the police and the tech crew from "Cops", or in the crack houses and heroin dens with the skanks and steel doors protecting a high that lasts a few seconds. Affirmative action is a ploy to lay the white man low. Well, how low can you go? Oh, that's right, Al Campanis already declared scientifically that however low white men go, niggahs don't float, so we must be on the bottom.

I'm actually "justified" in thinking that's how white folks think. My father was told he should study another language besides French because his lips were so thick. This decades after Leon Damas and Leopold Senghor gave the French language an entire new idiom, "Negritude." My mother once had a fiance who promised he could take her away "from all this." "What?" she asked her white devotee. "Why, from having to be colored." These are only two examples of how justice has been offered to my family. There's one more I mustn't leave out. A second-generation Polish teacher persuaded my parents that my sister, who ran like the wind or Wilma Rudolph, really should not pursue track and field because so many Negroes do that. Oh.

I wish Dinesh D'Souza had been in my front yard that night somebody white came with a firebomb. I wish Dinesh D'Souza had picked up one of his relative's bodies from the banks of the Little Geechee River or the side of an Alabama road with his genitals cut out, or just go to worship in a church, now ashes. Or, simply live off Hwy. 59 in Houston where some Anglo woman shouts, "Can't you niggahs just f_____ get out my way." We were crossing the street, my child and I, on the green light with the walking white neon person in plain view. My baby was not yet two, but she'd had her penultimate American experience.

———

"Niggahs, just get out my way." So we move downtown and they tear that down. We go to get work, but the work's moved outta town. They stopped the bus service because there were no more commuters. The suburbs were self-sufficient, except for day workers and menial laborers, and I figure we could get there anyway we could. After all, slaves got by on nothin', why can't you?

———

I don't wanna. So my escape from what is clearly a continuous assault on all my sensibilities is to talk myself out of it. Talk around the racism in English, Spanish, and French, enough to create a world to sustain me. I've found whatever I can call justice by forever returning to the root of a language, the design of a plantation, the workings of a sugar mill, the chants of street corner B-boys, the words of those before me—Garvey, Marti, Diop, Machel, and the images of Bearden, Barthé, Michaux. I have to scrape the bottoms of souls, dreams, nightmares, and syllables to taste what justice might possibly be.

SUSAN RICHARDS SHREVE

THE SILENT JUROR

The notice of John David Drewer's death of a heart attack at the filling station in Northern Virginia from which he apparently ran a drug operation was on the front page of the *Washington Post* the same day that a mummified Incan girl was put on view for the public at the National Geographic Building. Spring 1996.

The five-hundred-year-old Incan girl, frozen in time, grips the dress she had worn to the occasion of the sacrifice of her life—a ritual that must have honored her at the same time it protected her people, or she would not have been so dearly dressed.

The name John David Drewer did not capture my attention. His dying by the gas pump did, and so I read through the story. For several years in the 1980s, the gas station had been a suspected front for a large-scale drug operation, and though it was believed that John David Drewer was at its center, responsible for at least one drug-related killing if not more, no one except John Drewer's son had been arrested on any count. That son, the story said, was serving twenty-five years in prison for illegal possession and crossing state lines with four pounds of cocaine. The article didn't mention the name of the son, but I knew his name, Leroy Drewer III. I saw him clearly in my mind's eye, the defendant, age eighteen, small for a grown boy, small-boned with a quarter-sized patch of beard at the end of his chin and a stutter.

There was something about Leroy Drewer, some animal innocence or vulnerability that stays. I think of him, where he is now,
what is going on in his mind as he considers his father dying. Reading the newspaper account, I find myself imagining Leroy Drewer's
life in full—as if I must, as if I have a responsibility.

FROM THE D.C. JAIL, MAXIMUM SECURITY

What you need to understand is that I'm very sorry my father is dead.

*Last week on a Tuesday, when my mother came here to tell me, two weeks
after it happened, a heart attack in the filling station, no way for me to
know about it. But when she told me, I put my head down on the table and
cried like a baby.*

"What do you mean crying like that for nothing, Leroy?" she asked me.

"He is my father," I said.

*Plain and simple. That is the truth. He was my father and now I've
been having dreams waking me in the middle of the night, seeing him lying
on the asphalt beside the gas pump like they found him, his big arms, great
big thick arms—you should have seen them. You would have been impressed.*

The trial of Leroy Drewer III took place in criminal court of the
District of Columbia in late May 1990 and was, at its inception, ex-
pected to last three days. It was a clear-cut case for the prosecution.
That's what we expected.

I was selected to serve on the jury late in the morning after at
least thirty people had failed to qualify. It is difficult to assemble
twelve jurors who have not, among other things, been witnesses or
victims or relatives of victims of crime in Washington, D.C. The
jury finally chosen for Leroy Drewer's trial—nine blacks, three
whites—was not unrepresentative of the population of the city,
which is primarily black but also white and Hispanic with a small
number of Asians. I was the youngest of five women, juror #7. I remember all of the jurors, but when I think about the trial, five of
them in particular come to mind—all dissenters—and I plan to
count on them for this piece.

Mason Bridges. Age 36. Machinist. Reverend Billy Treeman.
Age 68. Minister First Baptist 16th Street. Thomas Brown. Age

45. Former electrician on disability. Evangeline Hurd. Age 71. Housewife. Mary Cable. Age 59. Retired Giant Food Store clerk. Juror #8.

Even now, I can feel her enormous silent presence beside me on the bench.

The trial itself took eight days. In reporting it, I take the liberty of condensing the story to testimony essential to the central argument that took place among us as we struggled towards a consensus. I should add that this narrative is not exact. It is rather a reconstruction of a sense of things for this one juror, a recognition of the mercurial nature of memory.

On the 18th of January 1990, Leroy Drewer III was arrested in Union Station in a sleeping compartment of the Miami-to-Washington Amtrak for illegal possession of four pounds of cocaine.

It was our charge as jurors to determine whether the defendant was guilty of the stated crime. This was my first trial, and I noted that on several occasions we were given information on the specifics of the accusation as if the court were accustomed to jurors with limited attention spans. Later I understood that we *had* to be reminded so we would not forget that our responsibility was to the specific construct of the law, that justice and the law are not interchangeable, that laws are written with a Hobbesian view of man in mind, to protect us from one another, that justice is a dream.

From the outset, I paid particular attention to Leroy Drewer as he sat next to his attorney, an extremely pale and anxious young man who leaned over his notes.

Leroy Drewer III—we learned later there had been no first or second—sat extremely straight, church straight, following the action in the courtroom exactly. From time to time he looked at the jurors, his eyes traveling down the line of us, fixing, I thought at the time, on me (although other jurors said later they'd felt the same thing). We did not make eye contact.

John David Drewer—now dead—was the fourth witness for the prosecution and appeared on the witness stand for the first time on the third day of the trial wearing an open-neck white shirt with gold chains. He seemed on first impression too young to be the father of a grown boy—clear-spoken and respectful—a reluctant witness but not deferential to the court.

DEFENSE: Do you know the defendant?

JDD: I do, sir. He is my son, Leroy Drewer, the third.

DEFENSE: You are aware that he was arrested on January 18, 1990, in the Amtrak train from Miami on charges of possession of four pounds of cocaine?

JDD: I am, sir.

DEFENSE: How did you learn of this?

JDD: I received a telephone call from the police in Washington that Leroy had been arrested. They asked me did I know what Leroy was doing in Miami.

DEFENSE: What did you tell the police?

JDD: I told the police I did not know that Leroy was in Miami. Monday was his day off from the filling station where he pumps gas, and he told me he was going to Philly to visit his grandmother.

DEFENSE: I understand that you drove the defendant to Union Station on Saturday evening to catch the train to Miami.

JDD: I did, sir, but I thought Leroy was catching the train to Philly.

DEFENSE: According to your son, you walked with him to the ticket counter and bought his ticket and then walked with him to the gate. Is that correct?

JDD: It is correct that I walked with him into the station, but I did not buy his ticket and I didn't go to the gate or I would've known the train he took was headed to Miami.

DEFENSE: According to the defendant, he had instruc-
            tions to pick up a package in a Miami parking
            lot.
JDD: I don't know anything about a package in
            Miami, sir.

Melvin Drewer, Leroy's uncle, took the stand after his brother.
He was older, skittish, less polite. He knew nothing about drugs, he
said, nothing about Leroy's trip to Miami, had heard nothing about
it until Leroy was in the slammer—Melvin's word—had been in
bed with the intestinal flu, too sick to work at the filling station he
owned with his brother.

"Leroy's had trouble with the law before," Melvin Drewer said.

"What kind of trouble?" the defense attorney asked.

"Stealing from the grocery store," Melvin said.

"For the record," the defense attorney said, in his quiet nervous
way, "this is the defendant's first offense."

There were many other witnesses—cousins and other uncles, a
grandmother and two employees of the filling station, and two
friends of Leroy's, one of whom worked the day shift with Leroy at
the gas station. But not one of them knew about Leroy Drewer's trip
to Miami. They all thought he had gone to Philly.

As the days progressed, it became perfectly clear to those of us
witnessing the trial—the judge, the lawyers, the visitors in the
courtroom, the jury—that John David Drewer was involved in a
drug operation with his brother Melvin and maybe others who also
testified ignorance of the crime, that the father had sent Leroy to
Miami with $4,000 to pick up a package containing four pounds of
cocaine, and that Leroy may or may not have known what he was
doing (although most certainly he knew he was doing something he
shouldn't be). When the defendant was called to the witness stand,
he shot up from his chair, straightened his jacket, and walked pur-
posefully with his head high, as if he were expecting a good conclusion to the proceedings. On the witness stand, he stood very

straight with his arms down at his sides facing the prosecutor directly, unflinching.

PROSECUTOR: Did you take a train from Washington, D.C., to Miami, Florida, on the 18th of January?

DEFENDANT: I did, sir.

PROSECUTOR: Did you pick up this package (submitted as evidence) in Miami and bring it back on the train to Washington, D.C.?

DEFENDANT: I did, sir.

PROSECUTOR: Did you know what the package contained?

DEFENDANT: No, sir.

PROSECUTOR: You had no idea?

DEFENDANT: No, sir.

PROSECUTOR: Where did you get this package?

DEFENDANT: I got it outside the Piggly Wiggly in northwest Miami on Glower Avenue.

PROSECUTOR: Who gave it to you?

DEFENDANT: A man in an orange baseball cap drinking a slurpee.

PROSECUTOR: What was his name?

DEFENDANT: I don't know his name, sir. I was told to say "my name is Leroy" if I saw a man in an orange baseball cap. So I did. I went to his car with him and he gave me a package and drove me into town.

PROSECUTOR: Was there an exchange?

DEFENDANT: I don't know what you mean, sir.

PROSECUTOR: Did it cost you anything to get the package?

DEFENDANT: Yes, sir. It cost me $4,000. I carried the money in an envelope in my sock.

PROSECUTOR: Where did you get $4,000?

DEFENDANT: From them.

PROSECUTOR: Who is them?

DEFENDANT: The people who wanted the package.

PROSECUTOR: Your father?

DEFENDANT: No, sir.

PROSECUTOR: Your Uncle Melvin?

DEFENDANT: No, sir.

PROSECUTOR: Will you say who them is, Mr. Drewer?

DEFENDANT: No, sir. I'd rather be dead.

The last night of the trial went so late they brought the jury dinner and we ate on the tables where the defense and prosecution had been sitting for the last eight days. Mary Cable sat in Leroy's seat. I remember that in particular. She was not a large woman but there was a sense of size about her, a kind of spiritual presence. She didn't speak at all, but I had the feeling that she knew things we didn't know. Even when her eyes were closed, you could tell she was attentive not only to the subject of Leroy Drewer but to each one of us. I, for one, wanted to please her.

Reverend Billy Treeman was chosen foreman of the jury and when we assembled in the deliberating room, he recommended an initial straw vote.

It was the first time we'd sat face to face around a table, the first time we'd spoken to one another, the first time any one of us had a real sense of another's point of view. No doubt the foreman believed as I did that we all agreed on a verdict and there would be no need for a discussion. But he had misjudged. We all had.

The vote was seven, guilty to five, not guilty.

The foreman shook his head.

"He was framed," Thomas Brown said. "Clear as day."

The foreman, Reverend Treeman, repeated the charge. "It's our duty to decide whether Leroy Drewer is guilty as charged."

"Innocent until proven guilty," Mason Bridges said.

"We have had eight days of proof," another juror said. "He was arrested with the cocaine. He was guilty of that. Right?" He looked around the table. "Right?"

I looked away.

"He was set up by his own kin and he's still a boy," Thomas Brown said. "You can hear the boy lingering in his voice."

Mary Cable made a low guttural sound in her throat, but her face was unreadable, her eyes half closed.

"His father is a snake," Mason Bridges said.

"He's a dealer," another juror said.

"I think his mother could've come to his defense," Thomas Brown said. "She is his mother after all."

"I think his father should be in jail for betrayal," Mason Bridges said.

"His father isn't on trial," Evangeline Hurd said. "We all know he was set up by his father, but that is not our job."

"Exactly," the Reverend foreman said. "Exactly so."

"Then what is our job, I'd like to know, if it isn't to give this boy a fair chance?" Thomas Brown said.

Mary Cable folded her arms and looked at Thomas Brown, maybe with disapproval or affection. I couldn't tell.

And so it went on into the night, the first time we met as a jury, late May, four days before Memorial Day.

At the end of the evening when we voted for a second time, I voted not guilty again.

I understood, of course, that our responsibility was to the law, and Leroy Drewer had broken the law. But I couldn't write the word guilty. It didn't seem the right conclusion.

Before the foreman announced the vote, Mason Bridges, braver than the rest of us, asked Mary Cable did she think Leroy was guilty or not. Her eyes rolled up towards the ceiling, she leaned back in her chair and shook her head.

"That's against the rules, Mr. Bridges," the foreman said, announcing the second vote, slightly altered—nine, guilty to three, not guilty.

We looked around the room to see who might have changed his or her mind. My guess was Evangeline Hurd or maybe Mason Bridges. He looked uncomfortable.

"Don't you all change your mind and vote guilty just because it's coming on a holiday and you want to get this over with," Thomas Brown said.

I left the building with Thomas Brown and Mary Cable. In the elevator we didn't look at one another or speak, although Thomas Brown did say under his breath just as the elevator doors opened, "I've been to trials before and I don't like this one."

It was almost midnight and because the area around the courthouse was not particularly safe, they had cabs waiting for us. I climbed into mine.

The other jurors climbed into their cabs, but I noticed that Mary Cable refused, walking off alone into the night towards the subway.

———

On the third day, I changed my vote to guilty.

We had been together in deliberation for twenty-four hours off and on. The vote had been taken six times. Seven to five, nine to three, eight to four, eight to four, nine to three, nine to three.

It was still nine to three after I changed my vote.

I looked around the room at Mary Cable, who was looking at me. I was sure she knew I had changed my vote.

"We're going to be here until we die," the foreman said wearily.

"I'm happy to die here," Thomas Brown said. "Leroy's counting on us."

By the fourth day, we were exhausted. Any clarity we had when we began to meet had slipped away, and we were beginning to have trouble remembering the particulars of the trial.

After lunch on the fourth day, the vote still nine to three, the conversation growing repetitive, the judge came into the room (which we were told was a rare occurrence).

He wanted to simplify our deliberation, he said. Once again, he repeated the specifics of the offense, reminding us that we were responsible not to our own sense of fairness but to the law.

"Are there any questions?" he asked.

"None," Mary Cable said. It was the first time she had spoken in four days.

"I'm getting out of here," one juror said after the judge left.

"So am I," another said. "I don't have time for sentimentalists."

"He was caught with four pounds of cocaine. Isn't that right? Aren't those the facts?" another said. "He was guilty of the crime, for chrissake."

"We aren't God," Mason Bridges said.

"I can't stand to send that boy to jail," Thomas Brown said. "I'll tell you right now that I'm prepared to stay here until Christmas, but I will not change my vote."

I noticed the room was suddenly too hot, unsettled, uncomfortable. I felt at risk. Mason Bridges, sitting on Thomas Brown's right, stood up. "I'm leaving now," he said. "I did my job and I'm going home." He shoved Thomas Brown in the shoulder and just as he started out the door, Mary Cable stood up and in a voice that reached around the room, called out, "Let us join hands and pray."

We stood obediently. There were no dissenters. Mason Bridges slipped back to his place between Thomas and Evangeline. We took hold of the hand on either side of us and bowed our heads as if the whole reason we'd come together was for the purpose of a prayer meeting.

"Dear Lord," she began. "Help us to make the right decision about Leroy. Help us to understand that we are only ordinary men and women capable of some things and not of others. We can't be responsible for justice. You are responsible for justice, Lord, and we cannot guess at your ways. Amen."

We all said "amen" and took our seats and sat in silence until the foreman asked did we wish to have any more discussion? He went around the room one by one. No, the answer was. We did not.

"Are you ready to vote?" he asked.

We nodded yes.

He passed the slips of paper for the seventh time in four days, and we sat without looking at one another while the votes were counted.

I do not believe any one of us was surprised.

"Twelve to zero," the foreman said. "Guilty."

I have often thought about that evening in an effort to understand what went on with all of us—with Thomas Brown and Mary Cable, with me particularly, how we could in the end settle so easily into a decision as if all along we'd been waiting on God.

We were, after all, the same mix of believers and nonbelievers as you no doubt would find in any random selection of twelve Americans.

I wonder was it Mary Cable with her astonishing voice? Was it her conviction, her own belief in God, that allowed us to relinquish our responsibility for justice? Or was it at the bottom *knowing* that we do not own our standards for judgment. If such a thing as justice is possible, it belongs to God and not to human beings, is written on our consciousness by God, and is, in any case, whatever our personal beliefs, out of our control.

FROM THE D.C. JAIL, MAXIMUM SECURITY

Listen Mama, don't you worry so much over me. I eat alright and I do my work and they say I'm behaving myself. I don't like getting beaten but it's no worse than Uncle Melvin used to do to me, and stop fussing about my father. He did what he had to do.

If you want to know, it's the jury I'm mad at. I looked at them up and down every day of that trial so they could catch my eye and know me for a God-fearing family boy who doesn't hurt anybody. They're the ones who put me in jail. Not my father and not Uncle Melvin.

And I'm no sacrifice in spite of what you say. I'm just a man serving time, no different than any other. Except at night I pray to God that I'll be released and I pray for you and I pray for my father on my hands and knees.

When the Incan fathers took their darling girl, dressed so beautifully in her handwoven costume, to the high cold mountains of Peru and asked her to kneel before them and smashed her skull, they must have honored her, believed her chosen, their treasured gift to their gods, their loss, their true sacrifice.

MISSISSIPPI

"THEY SHOULD HAVE KILLED ALL OF THEM"

I was raised in the South, in Memphis, Tennessee, which borders the state of Mississippi, where blacks systematically had been denied the right to vote for all but a few Reconstruction years immediately after the Civil War. Memphis is so connected to Mississippi that some of the Memphis suburbs are actually located in that state. Our downtown Hotel Peabody, where we white kids held our dances during high school, was immortalized by a Mississippi writer for its place in Mississippi's Delta plantation life. He wrote that "The Mississippi Delta begins in the lobby of the Peabody Hotel and ends on Catfish Row in Vicksburg." The rich cotton planters from Mississippi's Delta shopped in Memphis, partied at Memphis's annual Cotton Carnival, and stayed at the Hotel Peabody, dancing and dining in its elegance. The row of cotton brokers on Memphis's Front Street and its economy in general were ineluctably tied to Mississippi and its cotton plantations. But I was not so tied to Memphis.

My mother was born and raised in Memphis, growing up in her family's rooms above their dry goods store, playing with black children who lived side by side with white children in the neighborhood around their store. She was a true southerner with a lovely southern drawl. But I was born in Chicago, and we did not move to my mother's home city until 1946 when I was nine years old. I always felt like an outsider there, trying haltingly and often with embarrassment to learn the rituals and mores of this strange place.

One of my first memories of Memphis is the time my mother's black childhood friend, Bea Bunley, by then the wife of the owner of the shoe repair shop behind my grandparents' dry goods store, took me on the Crosstown bus from our house, where she had been helping us move in, to the furniture store my parents had opened next door to my grandparents' store. When we got on the bus, I followed her as she moved to a seat near the back. She pushed me toward the front of the bus and told me to go sit up there and not with her. I was upset to be separated from her on this big bus in this new city where I knew no one. When I tried again to go back and sit with her, she forced me to return, alone, to a seat in the front. I was hurt and bewildered. Later, when we got to my parents' store, they explained to me that Memphis had some rigid rules of segregation. My parents also made clear to me their disapproval of these rules.

As I grew up in Memphis I learned the rules. Blacks called white men, even young white boys like me, "sir." I saw the separate white and colored water fountains in our downtown department stores. My younger sister was jealous that she couldn't drink the beautiful, rainbow water that she imagined came from the "colored" fountain. Blacks could not enter the front door of Memphis's elegant, chandeliered, downtown Malco Theater where we went every Saturday afternoon to see the newest movie. They had to go through a back door and climb the long stairway to the colored balcony. The Memphis Zoo, across the street from my junior high school, was open to blacks only on Thursday, "colored" day. Our downtown library did not set aside even one day a week for blacks. Blacks were not allowed in the white swimming pools or at the big lake and picnic grounds in Mississippi my uncle took us kids to on weekends. And, of course, there were no blacks in our white schools and no discussions about any of these rules and practices.

Memphis also had rigid rules for Jews that made me, a Jewish boy, feel even more of an outsider in my new southern home. My schools, Snowden Junior High School and Memphis Central High School, had fraternities, but Jews were not allowed in. We had our own separate all-Jewish fraternities and sororities, which became the focal point for all our parties and athletics, with all-Jewish dances and all-Jewish intrafraternity basketball and baseball leagues.

One night, during one of our Jewish fraternity meetings, I learned for the first time that only a few years earlier the Nazis had killed millions of Jews, including young Jewish boys our age, and used their skins to make lampshades. I was terrified, but I do not recall talking with my parents, or anyone else, about the Holocaust. Of course, this too was never taught or mentioned in school. But I do remember my fears, and my nightmares in high school, of Nazis marching down my street to drag me from my bedroom, powerless to protect myself from torture and death.

During college in the East, I read the book *Exodus* and learned that in 1948 young Jewish boys, even eleven-year-old boys, had fought for Israel to help create a homeland where Jews would not be outsiders or powerless to defend themselves. I calculated that I had been eleven years old in 1948, and wished I had been there to fight alongside them. I remember feeling I had missed out on my one chance to strike back at the powerlessness I felt as a Jew, as an outsider, as a minority, as a stranger in a strange land.

During my second year in law school, I saw on the nightly TV news four black college freshmen in Greensboro, North Carolina, sit down at a Woolworth's lunch counter reserved for "whites only" and start a revolutionary movement that led to similar sit-ins all throughout the South. The country's attention was riveted on these young nonviolent students, taunted and tormented by angry whites while they stoically sought service at segregated lunch counters. Whenever they tried, the police would arrive and arrest and jail them, accusing them of breaching the peace.

I wrote my senior law school thesis on their new sit-in movement and got myself deep into their new struggle for freedom. I concluded that the best way to change the South was through the ballot box. I felt when blacks got the right to vote, the politicians would make sure the lunch counters were open to all.

It was 1961. Kennedy had just been inaugurated as president and was ready to use fully the new powers Congress had just given the Civil Rights Division of the U.S. Department of Justice to prohibit discrimination against blacks seeking to register to vote. That was where I wanted to be. I had missed out when the Jews fought for their independence in 1948. Because I was a Jew, or an outsider to the South, or for some other reason I still cannot fathom, I identified with the blacks in their new fight, and I did not want to miss out this time.

Fortunately for me the Civil Rights Division hired me. I soon found myself in Selma and other little towns in Alabama, negotiating against people like Snag Andrews, the Speaker of the Alabama House of Representatives, who had gone to the University of Alabama with my mother; and in the segregated parishes of Louisiana; and in Savannah, Georgia, where my law school classmate and fellow member of Harvard Law School's Southern Club told me I should leave his city and his state. But most of the time I spent in deepest Mississippi.

When I first went to Mississippi, I was scared. I had fears of being beaten, even killed. My first trips to the Delta emphasized for me the precarious position of anyone in Mississippi who might try to change Mississippi's ways of dealing with its blacks. I went to Senatobia, Mississippi, to visit an uncle who owned the biggest department store in the county. I told him what I was doing and asked if he could give me some information about how his county kept blacks from registering to vote. He quickly told me he was a member of the White Citizens Council, a group of white businessmen organized in the Delta to insure the continuation of segregation after the Supreme Court decided that separate but equal schools for blacks were unconstitutional. He felt that, because he was a Jew, he was always suspect in the eyes of his Mississippi neighbors, so he had to be one of the first to join their local White Citizens Council. He would not help me in any way. After I was ushered out he immediately drove to Memphis to see my rabbi to persuade him to tell my family that I should be assigned to Georgia or Alabama where I would not cause a backlash against the Jews of Mississippi and Memphis.

The same thing happened when I went to Clarksdale, Mississippi, and called on a German Jewish refugee from the Holocaust who was teaching German in the local junior college. I assumed he would be sympathetic to the plight of blacks being mistreated by the political powers of Mississippi. When I asked for information about his county, he refused to help and went right to the sheriff's office to let him know I had been in town.

But other Jews in the South spoke up bravely against the treatment of blacks. During one of the Civil Rights Division's first trials in federal district court in Alabama against a registrar who had discriminated against black voter applicants, the government counsel subpoenaed white people to testify that, when they went to register, they did not have to pass the kind of test given to black applicants. I was sitting in the courtroom during the testimony from one of these white witnesses who happened to be Jewish and spoke with a foreign accent. The federal district judge left the bench during this testimony and wandered over to the people sitting in the courtroom. I was a lowly assistant on this case, so he did not know who I was. I overheard him tell one of the local white political leaders, "They should have killed all of them in Germany."

"OUR COLORED GENTRY"

The federal judge who would decide the fate of the government's voter rights cases in Mississippi was William Harold Cox. Harold Cox had been born into the Mississippi power structure in Sunflower County, in the heart of the rich plantation, cotton-growing Delta of the Old South. His father was the sheriff of Sunflower County, the "high sheriff" as blacks referred to him, and the most powerful and feared political figure in the county. Harold Cox's boyhood friend from Sunflower County, Jim Eastland, the son of a prosperous cotton planter in Sunflower County, would later force President Kennedy to make Harold Cox one of his first judicial appointments. Jim Eastland, by then the Chairman of the Senate Judiciary Committee, refused to clear Kennedy's nomination of Thurgood Marshall to the United States Court of Appeals for the Second Circuit unless the President agreed to nominate Harold Cox to the District Court in Mississippi. The story is that Jim Eastland told the Kennedys: "I'll give you the nigger and you give me Cox."

In the first voter rights case tried by the Civil Rights Division in Mississippi before the newly appointed Judge Cox, the government proved, among other things, that white voter applicants were registered by the deputy clerks in the registrar's office, often without even having to fill out the application form required by Mississippi law, while all black applicants were required to see the registrar in person and still were not allowed to register to vote. When the government asked Judge Cox at least to order the deputies to process the black applicants, Judge Cox lectured the government counsel about blacks in Mississippi:

> I think the colored people brought that on themselves. I
> am thoroughly familiar with some of the conduct, with some
> of our colored gentry, and I am not surprised at Mr. Lynd's
> [the registrar's] reaction, to what he stated in the record
> [that he would not permit the white women deputies to
> deal with black applicants] . . . although you folks up
> North don't understand what he is talking about. I don't
> expect you to, but I do. I understand exactly what he is
> talking about, and I think he did exactly right in taking
> these things on himself. And he said he could not afford to
> pay any male help. He has to use girls in there and those
> girls did not want to be subjected to those things, and that
> is understandable.

In another case around the same time, Judge Cox instructed another northern lawyer about the blacks he knew so much about: "I think the court could take judicial notice of the illiteracy that is prevalent among colored people; and I do know that of my own knowledge. And the intelligence of colored people don't compare ratio-wise to white people. I mean, that is just a matter of common knowledge."

"FIT SUBJECTS FOR THE PENITENTIARY"

I had my own troubles with Judge Cox, even though I was not one of those northerners ignorant of southern ways when I tried the Clarke County, Mississippi, voting case before him. I was twenty-five years old and only a year and a half out of law school. I was nervous as I began our case. Judge Cox, a big, imposing man, was un-smiling, severe, angry, and definitely unimpressed by me. I put the defendant registrar, A. L. Ramsey, a thin, frail eighty-two-year-old man, on the stand. Under cross-examination he testified he had reg-istered "practically all" of the 5,000 white persons on the registra-tion rolls, and that it had been the practice from "time immemor-ial" for white people to register for each other—husbands for wives, parents for children, brothers for sisters, and politicians for white voters. White people could register by proxy and did not have to take any test. Indeed, they did not even have to go to town to sign the registration book. An FBI handwriting expert testified that there were 1,500 instances where groups of two or more signatures on the registration book were written by one person. In one case one person had registered for fourteen different people. The testimony of the FBI expert alone proved that at least 30 percent of the 5,000 registered white voters had someone else register for them.

Mr. Ramsey candidly admitted he treated black persons differ-ently. He said he invariably refused to register them during his nine years as registrar when the black leaders of the county came in to register to vote "two or three at a time, or three or four, or one or two," including Samuel Owens, who had been the principal of Clarke County's black school for fifty-five years:

> I would always just tell them that I wasn't going to refuse
> them the opportunity to register but then I would just like
> for us to consider this matter, that due to the fact that they
> were having trouble in other parts of the country and that

we folks here in Mississippi, white and colored, were getting along together and they were our friends and we were
their friends and weren't going to have any trouble either
way, and then I just suggested to them they go back home
and consider this matter and think it over and come back
later.

He only decided to let blacks apply to register about the time
the government sued him. But he did not let them register the way
whites had, by simply signing the registration book in person or by
proxy. Instead they had to take a test and interpret the Mississippi
Constitution. The county's black principal got a section to interpret
that even Judge Cox said the "Supreme Court of Mississippi has had
considerably difficulty with."

It had not been easy to get the Clarke County black witnesses
to come to court. One of them, George Cotton, the President of
the Negro Benevolent Assurance Company, an intelligent businessman and framer well respected by the white people in Clarke
County, had missed an earlier pretrial hearing. He'd been visited
by a white man in the county who warned him that he better find
a way not to go to the hearing. So he fell off his tractor and had to
be hospitalized. After the pretrial hearing, I had gone by to see
him to tell him I still would need him to testify at the full trial
before Judge Cox. He said he'd try and come. I looked him in the
eye as we sat on his porch, grinned a bit, and told him I really
wanted him to come. He put his hands in the pockets of his over-
alls, looked my way, and said "I'll try and be there." I finally told
him, "Mr. Cotton. Let me read this subpoena to you. It says 'You
are hereby commanded to appear'—It doesn't say please." He
laughed—and came to the trial.

During the second day of the trial, Judge Cox made the com-
ment from the bench that there was "very substantial evidence of
discrimination against Negroes." That was an amazing concession
by the man who represented the Mississippi white power structure.
I made sure the wire services covering the trial had heard what
Judge Cox said, and I was proud of what we had accomplished in

the trial so far when his quote made headlines in Mississippi's major newspapers the next morning.

During the trial the next day, Judge Cox gave the newspapers a new headline. He looked down at me from the bench and sternly announced that he believed two of the Clarke County blacks who testified about the registrar's discrimination against them had lied: "I want to hear from the Government about why this court shouldn't require this Negro, Rev. W. G. Goff and his companion Kendrick to show cause why they shouldn't be bound over to await action of a grand jury for perjury. . . . I think they ought to be put under about a $3,000 bond each to await the action of a grand jury. . . . I think they are fit subjects for the penitentiary." Cox's tactics worked. The headlines in the major Mississippi paper the next morning was "Perjury Charge Faces Negroes in Clarke County Voter Case—Judge Says He Thinks Minister, One Other 'Lied' Against Ramsey."

After the FBI conducted a thorough investigation of the testimony of Reverend Goff and Mr. Kendrick, we informed Judge Cox there was "no basis for a perjury prosecution." So Judge Cox persuaded a private Clarke County lawyer to pursue perjury charges against the two Clarke County black witnesses before a state grand jury. The local lawyer filed two affidavits with the local justice of the peace, and Goff and Kendrick were arrested, jailed, and placed under a $3,000 property bond each, exactly as Judge Cox had suggested during the Clarke County trial. Goff and Kendrick spent two days in jail before they were able to make bond. The Clarke County grand jury then indicted them for committing perjury in Judge Cox's federal court in violation of the laws of the state of Mississippi.

———

Back in Washington, I buried myself in the Justice Department's fifth floor library—under the Depression-era WPA paintings depicting intolerance, brute force, greed, ambition, red tape, magic, justice tempered by mercy—searching for some way out for them. I found only one case, in all of our country's history, where a state

court prosecutor had tried to convict someone for perjury committed in a federal court. The decision held that perjury in a federal
court could only be a federal crime. Based on this case, the Justice
Department immediately sued in the Federal District Court for
the Southern District of Mississippi to prohibit Mississippi's prosecution of Reverend Goff and Mr. Kendrick. Because of Judge
Cox's direct involvement in this matter, the suit was assigned to
the other federal district judge in the Southern District, Judge
Sidney Mize.

To our relief, Judge Mize held that he was bound by federal
precedent to rule that a state could not prosecute for perjury in a
federal court. He ordered the state of Mississippi not to proceed
with their trial. Unfortunately, Judge Cox would not let that end
the matter. He ordered the U.S. Attorney in Jackson, Mississippi,
to seek a federal criminal indictment of them from a federal grand
jury.

When the U.S. Attorney refused to do so, Judge Cox arranged
for the private Clarke County lawyer to appear before a federal
grand jury, which then indicted Reverend Goff and Mr. Kendrick.
When the U.S. Attorney refused to sign the indictments, Judge
Cox held him in contempt of court and ordered him jailed. He also
ordered the Acting Attorney General of the United States, Nicholas
Katzenbach, to show cause why he too should not be held in contempt of court.

Eventually the Fifth Circuit—the federal appellate court for
Mississippi and the other Deep South states—in a four-to-three
vote reversed Judge Cox's contempt order against the U.S. Attorney
in Jackson, Mississippi, who had courageously refused to sign the
criminal indictments of Reverend Goff and Mr. Kendrick. The
Supreme Court declined to reverse the Fifth Circuit decision. But
the damage had been done. Blacks already knew from experience
that they had no hope for justice in Mississippi's state courts. Now,
with Judge Cox's active intervention against black witnesses who
appeared in his court in these voting cases, even a federal court was
not safe.

"IT'S NOT RIGHT FOR ANYONE
TO BE SEEN AS AN ANIMAL"

Despite Judge Cox's hostility to the efforts of blacks in Mississippi to register to vote, the government's voter rights cases continued to be assigned to him. This made it difficult to encourage black witnesses to come forth and testify in his court. In one case, a black schoolteacher was not rehired after she gave an affidavit to the government to use in a voter rights lawsuit against the registrar in her home county. We brought a new lawsuit in federal court to force the county to rehire her. We needed the testimony from one of her fellow teachers who knew that the real reason she was not rehired was her effort to register to vote. When I went to see this black teacher, he was in New York attending summer school at New York University in Greenwich Village and living in Harlem. I made a trip into Harlem to try and persuade him to come forward and tell the truth about the firing to Judge Cox back in Mississippi. The taxi driver who took me to Harlem refused to leave the wide cross street to drive me down the narrow street to where this witness was living. I got out at the corner and warily walked down the long street to find the witness.

He let me in to the dingy room he was renting for the summer, but he immediately went back to his chair at a small table and continued to study his math books under a ceiling light bulb hanging over his head. My bosses at the Justice Department had arranged for Thurgood Marshall, Martin Luther King Jr., and Attorney General Bobby Kennedy to call him, to ask him to tell me what had happened in Mississippi. I sat with him for hours, but he would not talk with me about the case. He knew he had to go back to Mississippi at the end of the summer to resume his teaching position, and he knew how little power the government had to protect him. As it began to get dark outside, I became nervous that I would not be able to get a cab to pick me up and get me back to white New York. As I thought about my own fear as a white man in black Harlem, I began to understand a little better how frightened this black teacher felt in the white world of Mississippi, at the mercy of whatever the white folks wanted to do to him.

Judge Cox ruled there was not enough proof that the purpose of not rehiring the teacher was to deprive her or other blacks of their right to vote. The Fifth Circuit, based on the limited evidence we were able to produce, had to agree with Judge Cox on this one.

But the government was able to provide some protection for a black student who tried to help black persons register to vote in another Mississippi county. In Walthall County, John Hardy, a young black college student from Nashville, Tennessee, along with some other students set up a voter registration school to teach local blacks how to register. For three weeks they conducted classes for several hours a day, teaching from twenty-five to fifty Walthall County residents each evening how to fill out registration forms and explain sections of the Mississippi Constitution. Finally, John Hardy accompanied the first five blacks to try and register to vote in Walthall County. At that time, none of the county's 2,490 black persons of voting age were registered to vote, while a substantial majority of 4,536 voting age white persons were registered. The first five black applicants were rejected, as were the three who tried the next time, and the one who tried the next time. The next effort, by two blacks accompanied by John Hardy, marked the last time blacks would try and register in Walthall County for a long time.

An elderly black man, Mose McGee, had been in town on that last day and had seen what had happened to John Hardy and the two black applicants. I found Mose McGee way back in the hills, plowing his fields behind a mule with the plow lines hitched over his shoulders. He was embarrassed for me to see him like that. He did not utter a single word. He just unhitched himself from his plow, went into his shack, cleaned up, and then came out. He said, "It's not right for anyone to be seen as an animal. I want you to see me as a human being."

He wanted to tell me what he had seen in town that day. He wanted blacks to get the right to vote so they could force the county supervisors to pave his dirt road and the dirt roads that led to other black people's homes like they paved the roads to white men's property. He said his dirt road became impassably muddy when the rains came. One day a black neighbor's baby got sick. No doctor could get up the road to them. And they couldn't drive out to get to the doctor. So he had bundled the baby up and walked over the hills, for miles and miles, to get to town. The baby died in his arms before he got there.

Mose McGee said John Hardy had accompanied Mrs. Edith Simmons Peters, a sixty-three-year-old black woman who owned an eighty-acre farm, and Lucius Wilson, a sixty-two-year-old black man who owned a seventy-acre farm, to register to vote. When they got to the registrar's office, he refused to allow them to apply. When the registrar saw John Hardy, he went into his office, got a gun from his desk, and ordered him to leave the office. As John Hardy turned to leave, the registrar followed him and struck him on the back of the head with his gun, saying, "Get out of here you damn son-of-a-bitch and don't come back in here."

John Hardy, bleeding from the head, staggered out of the building, helped by Mrs. Peters and Lucius Wilson, where he was soon met by the sheriff. When he told the sheriff what had happened, the sheriff pointed to Lucius Wilson and said, "If that boy wants to register he know how to go down to that courthouse and he don't need you to escort him. You don't have a bit of business in the world down there." Then the sheriff arrested John Hardy "for disturbing the peace and bringing an uprising among the people." When John Hardy tried to explain his side of the story, the sheriff said, "Don't give me none of your head, boy, or I will beat you within an inch of your life." John Hardy was put in the Walthall County jail, but that night, because feeling about the incident was running high in the community, he was transferred to a jail in another county and then released the next day on bond to stand trial in Walthall County for disturbing the peace.

The Justice Department filed a lawsuit in federal court to stop the state court prosecution of John Hardy. The government argued that, even if Hardy were to be acquitted, the prosecution itself would effectively intimidate blacks in the exercise of their right to vote in violation of federal law. Judge Cox had no difficulty denying the motion: "In the argument it is asserted that the trial of the case tomorrow will irreparably damage the United States in deterring colored people in Walthall County from registering. The statement is without any substantial support on the record before the Court and appears as a non sequitur."

When the government appealed, the Fifth Circuit ordered Judge Cox to prohibit the state's trial. In their opinion, the judges of the Fifth Circuit quoted approvingly from the government's argument that injunctive relief was not a "non sequitur" but a necessity to protect the rights of all those black citizens in Walthall County who were qualified to register and vote:

> On the basis of the record in this Court and in view of the conditions and circumstances prevailing in Mississippi, it is most unlikely that, if the appellees [the state of Mississippi] are allowed to proceed with Mr. Hardy's trial, further Negro registration will take place. The blunt truth is that it can really not be expected that Negroes who have lived all their lives under the white supremacy conditions which exist in that area of Mississippi will continue their efforts to register and otherwise exercise their rights and privileges of citizenship if in addition to being threatened and beaten, they will also be prosecuted in state court with all that such a prosecution entails.

"NOT INTERESTED IN REGISTERING TO VOTE"

Later Judge Cox issued an opinion rejecting our request that he order the Walthall County registrar to cease discriminating against black voter applicants like the two elderly black persons who accompanied John Hardy to the registrar's office. Judge Cox found that virtually all the 4,536 white persons of voting age in Walthall County were registered to vote, while "at the time of the trial only two negroes were registered" out of 2,490 black persons of voting age. But Judge Cox held that "such imbalance in registration was occasioned solely by reason of the fact that negroes have not been interested in registering to vote and very few have ever bothered to apply to register prior to 1957; whereas white people have been intensely interested in voting in elections in that county."

Of course, there was the additional evidence that the registrar had hit John Hardy on the head with a gun when he brought two elderly blacks in to register. Didn't that help explain the lack of interest in voting that Judge Cox was so certain about? Judge Cox ruled, "That incident did not frighten or deter any negro in the county from registering or attempting to register if he desired to do so."

Judge Cox did agree that the overwhelming evidence at the trial demonstrated that blacks who tried to register were discriminated against. He concluded, "The practice of the former registrar (Byrd) who died in the summer of 1961, was not to register negro citizens. John Q. Wood [the current registrar] was elected to the office on the promise to the citizens to follow the same course but he said that he had found that impossible and did not intend to try to do so." Instead, when he did let blacks apply, Judge Cox found he "assign[ed] white people easy sections of the Constitution to construe and helped them to do so; while he assigned negroes more difficult sections of the Constitution to copy and never helped them." In short, Judge Cox held that "most, if not all" of the black applicants "during the past six year period . . . have been discriminated against."

But the important question was whether Judge Cox would find this discrimination was pursuant to "a pattern or practice." Such a legal finding would empower the Department of Justice to seek the appointment of a federal voting referee for Walthall County. Judge Cox held, "There is no need or necessity for any finding by the Court as to a pattern or practice." Why not? "There were relatively so few negroes who applied to register to vote that it would be difficult if not impossible to make any determination on that question under the circumstances in this case."

Judge Cox then devised his own remedy for the discrimination against black applicants in Walthall County. He ordered the registrar "to desist from helping or making help available or allowing any applicant to receive help." And he then ordered the registrar to put forty-one sections of the Mississippi Constitution in a jar and to select them at random for new applicants. To preclude anyone, that is the blacks not yet registered, from studying these sections beforehand, he also ordered that "the identity of these [forty-one] sections shall not be revealed to anybody at any time for any purpose."

The Department of Justice continued to pursue these voter discrimination cases, county by county, case by case, but it was obvious there had to be a quicker, more effective way than battling Judge Cox and the Mississippi legislature while they constantly erected new hurdles to black voter registration. The Department of Justice decided to sue to invalidate the Mississippi registration requirements in their entirety.

When Judge Cox and another Mississippi judge from the Fifth Circuit dismissed the government's case, Judge Cox again emphasized the fact, clearly known to him, that blacks in Mississippi, from 1890 at least until the election of President Kennedy in 1960, were not interested in registering to vote. He wrote, "This court judicially knows that Negroes never manifested any substantial interest in registering or voting in Mississippi prior to a direct appeal to them from President Kennedy to do so."

Judge Cox also was not happy to see that blacks, now encouraged to register to vote, were doing so in large numbers. The day after he wrote of his own judicial knowledge of the long voting lethargy of blacks, he exploded over the efforts of two hundred blacks to register to vote in Madison County. From the bench he announced: "It appears these niggers went to church and were whipped into a frenzy by a leather-lunged preacher. Then they gathered in the streets like a massive dark cloud and descended on the clerk. I don't know who is telling these niggers they can get in line and push people around, acting like a bunch of chimpanzees?" The headline in the Jackson, Mississippi, newspaper the next morning was, "Race Agitators Lashed in U.S. Court Hearings."

In that same month, the Fifth Circuit reversed Judge Cox in the Clarke County voter discrimination case in which Reverend Goff and Mr. Kendrick had testified. The Fifth Circuit held that Judge Cox's finding that there was no pattern or practice of discrimination by the registrar, who had admitted blacks had been denied the right to register from "time immemorial," was "clearly erroneous." As for Judge Cox's assertion that blacks were not interested in registering to vote, the Fifth Circuit's Judge Brown dryly noted in a footnote, "The fact that more did not attempt to register might be explained by the fact that the discrimination against those who did try probably discouraged others from trying."

AN UNLIKELY HERO

Within a few months, Martin Luther King Jr.'s efforts to dramatize the discrimination against black voter applicants in Selma, Alabama, would galvanize the nation into more drastic and effective action to end the refusal of southern registrars to let blacks register to vote and to take these cases out of the hands of judges like Judge Cox.

Congress passed the 1965 Voting Rights Act. It suspended voter registration tests and devices in any state or political subdivision that used such tests as of November 1, 1964, and in which less than half of the eligible adults were registered to vote in the November 1964 presidential election. In those states and counties, which included all of Mississippi, the Department of Justice could send in federal voting examiners to register voters without requiring that they take the state's voter registration tests and without having to ask judges like Judge Cox to make any findings or enter any order.

Judge Cox, unwittingly, had been instrumental in the passage of this new law. As Jack Bass wrote in his book *Unlikely Heroes* (the title referred to the courageous judges on the Fifth Circuit, and not to Judge Cox):

> In the final analysis, Cox played a role comparable to that of Bull Connor in Birmingham [with his police dogs attacking young black students shown on TV news throughout the country] and Sheriff Jim Clark at Selma [with his gassing of the Selma marchers similarly on the nightly TV news] in creating a climate for Congress to act. Although

Cox wasn't alone as an obstructionist judge in voting cases, his blatantly outrageous conduct and publicized antics probably contributed to passage of the Voting Rights Act by helping make Congress conclude that nothing less would solve the problem.

The fight for the right of blacks to register to vote did change things in Mississippi. The percentage of blacks registered to vote in Mississippi jumped from 6.7 percent prior to the 1965 Voting Rights Act to 59.8 percent two years after the act became law. But Mississippi, like Judge Cox, did not change so fast. After 1965, Mississippi shifted its tactics from denying blacks the right to vote to preventing blacks from winning elections. Among other steps, Mississippi gerrymandered the congressional district lines to prevent the election of a black to Congress, created large, multimember state legislative districts to dilute black votes, and switched to at-large elections for county offices to prevent the election of black candidates. Nevertheless, some blacks were elected to Congress— Mike Espy became the first black Congressmember to represent the Delta—and to the state legislature and to county offices.

HATTIESBURG

I recently returned to Hattiesburg, Mississippi, in Forrest County, thirty-two years after my last efforts there on behalf of the federal government. We had tried a voting rights case in Hattiesburg back in the 1960s before Judge Cox, and for me that case had been particularly painful. I had gotten to know the leader of the black community in Forrest County, Vernon Dahmer, a strong, powerfully built man, a successful businessman, farmer, and community leader, respected by blacks and whites throughout the county. Back in the 1950s he had helped raise $2,500 to finance a lawsuit against the local registrar for discriminating against black voter applicants. The suit was lost in the federal court.

In 1961 the federal government filed one of the first suits under the 1960 Civil Rights Act to order the new registrar of Forrest

County not to discriminate against black applicants. This case was assigned to Judge Cox as one of his first cases as a federal judge, and not surprisingly he delayed the government's efforts and never gave the relief requested. Eventually the judges of the Fifth Circuit ordered Judge Cox to register specific black applicants discriminated against by the Forrest County registrar, including Vernon Dahmer and one of his sons, and then when the 1965 Voting Rights Act passed, blacks of Forrest County began to be registered in large numbers.

But there was still an 1890 Mississippi requirement that voters had to have receipts for two years of poll taxes at $2 a year before they could vote. In January 1966, Vernon Dahmer announced on the radio that he would provide poll tax receipts for blacks who wanted to pay their poll taxes at his country store rather than risk going to town to pay poll taxes at the sheriff's office. The Ku Klux Klan responded to this last effort of Vernon Dahmer to get blacks the right to vote in Forrest County by ordering his house fire-bombed in the night. While shooting at the Klan attackers, to allow his wife and children to escape from the back of their burning house, Vernon Dahmer's lungs were seared by smoke and flame. He died in the hospital the next day, but not before he was able to tell a reporter for the Hattiesburg paper that "what happened to us last night can happen to anybody, white or black. At one time I didn't think so, but I have changed my mind."

Vernon Dahmer's last words warning white people that they may be just as vulnerable as the blacks of Mississippi reminded me of a quote from Martin Niemoller, a leader of the Confessing Church in Germany, who voted for the Nazi party in 1933. By 1938, he was in a concentration camp. After the war, he is believed to have said, "In Germany, the Nazis came for the Communists, and I didn't speak up because I wasn't a Communist. Then they came for the Jews, and I didn't speak up because I wasn't a Jew. Then they came for the trade unionists, and I didn't speak up because I wasn't a trade unionist. Then they came for the Catholics, and I didn't speak up because I was a Protestant. Then they came for me, and by that time there was no one left to speak for me."[1]

After Vernon Dahmer's death, the previously silent white people of Hattiesburg spoke up. A number of the Klan members who killed Vernon Dahmer were caught by local law enforcement officers working with FBI agents from Mississippi, prosecuted for murder and arson by Hattiesburg's own district attorney, convicted by local Hattiesburg jurors, and sentenced to life imprisonment by a local Hattiesburg judge. Thirty-two years later I could see significant changes in Hattiesburg. Now the senior city judge is black, the senior representative to the state legislature is black, the chief deputy sheriff is black, and two of the five city councilors are black. The city has numerous black medical and other professional people, and a few blacks live next door to whites in new homes in some of Hattiesburg's wealthiest neighborhoods. The Waffle House even had black and white waitresses waiting on the customers, and no one but me seemed to think that was anything out of the ordinary.

Of course, vestiges of the Old South still remain. Many white children attend private white schools rather than go to public schools with black children. At Hattiesburg's new airport, I could not help but notice the paper cup dispenser next to the cold water fountain, for those who still refuse to drink from the same spigot as black people. More ominously, there recently has been an epidemic of black church burnings throughout the South, eerily reminding us again of the 1960s when the Klan firebombed black churches and Jewish synagogues in Mississippi.

As a young boy in Memphis, I had nightmares of Nazis coming down my street at night to get me. For the blacks in Mississippi in the 1960s, like Vernon Dahmer, the Klan did come in the night to get him and his family. But many people, including the federal government using the power of the law, as well as poor black farmers like Mose McGee who demanded dignity and refused to allow himself to be seen as an animal, spoke up and changed things for all of those living in the South, black and white.

---

1.   Martin Sleeper, Margot Stern Strom, and Henry C. Zabierek, "Facing History and Ourselves Resource Book," *Educational Leadership* 48 (Nov. 1990): 206.

DANIEL J. WIDEMAN

FREE PAPERS

If a word burns on your tongue, let it burn.
PERSIAN PROVERB

Whenever somebody says justice, I always hear the homonym "just us"; as in "justice comes down on 'just us' black folks." Regardless of the context or the speaker's intent, I hear it. Despite the fact some part of me always thought the double entendre was facile, and that its adoption by the hip-hop generation has rendered it a pop-culture cliché, it still flashes through my mind. The reaction so deeply ingrained now it borders on instinct. Pavlovian response. "Justice" out of anybody's mouth an irksome, tinkling bell; and though I can anticipate it, I can never quite suppress the smirk that rises to my lips. Whenever the word comes up in an ethnically mixed gathering, my eyes scan the room for color—searching out dark faces that might dare to meet my furtive grin with a knowing wink; looking for the faintest flush in a pair of white cheeks, a hint of uncomfortable redness so I can imagine "they" hear the hypocrisy too, are in on the joke; recognize, even if only silently, the absurdity *we* see in the blindfolded lady primly holding up scales.

Sitting down to think seriously about justice, I guess I was a little surprised when the old "justice-just us" refrain began marching like a mantra through my mind. I had been intending to write about the politics of imprisonment in America; to explore questions

like what constitutes "imprisoned space"? Does it extend beyond
the bars and locks of prison walls, beyond institutional confine-
ment? Are there people "locked up" in territory officially called
free? Does a jail-by-any-other-name stink as bad? The stories I was
searching for when I mapped out this essay were those that might
illustrate how the politics of naming space, of constructing narratives of freedom and incarceration, crime and punishment, determine who gets "imprisoned" in America. I hadn't planned on discussing what I considered at root a fairly silly inside joke. But the
bell kept ringing, too loud to ignore.

"Just us!" is the most obvious and immediate story buried in the
word "justice" for me—the story I have to acknowledge and unpack
before I can begin to tell any others. It hangs around in my head because like all phrases that gain sufficient currency to become pat, at
some level it *works*. A cliché begins as a story told well enough to
appropriate. It registers a truth enough people recognize that they
repeat it reflexively to each other, somewhere along the way overlooking or getting comfortable with the fact that all the eccentrici-
ties, the complex contradictions of their individual experiences
might get lost, subsumed by communal code.

"Justice" the call. "Just us!" the response. It is not a reply born
of resignation; not the self-pitying wail of the persecuted. "Just us!"
is a subversive reconfiguration; the announcement of an alternative
text. A defiant challenge to reconcile the hollow sound of a noble
abstraction with the resonant fury of unjust discrimination. "Just
us!" is one of the titles black folk have invented and adopted to
frame our collective narrative of justice in America. It affirms the
particular exclusivity of our experience here, before, and beyond the
law. Yet it is also inclusive, an expansive invitation. One implicit
message of "just us!" is the potential for amelioration through con-
gregation. If "justice" is the long arm of the law wielding the whip
that cracks across "just our" backs, then if you been done wrong,
you're family. Your story is ours. We've heard it before, know the
intricacies of your pain, sing it every day. "Just us!" is permission to
tune up and lend your voice to the throng.

A dog starv'd at his master's gate
predicts the ruin of the state.
WILLIAM BLAKE

A couple times a year, for nearly ten years, I drove past the crumbling, sand-blasted signs on I-10 announcing the "Gila Indian Reservation & Museum" without stopping. Truth be told, I barely registered the existence of such a place. It never found a way to permeate the peculiar topography of the Arizona desert I've constructed and carried around in my head. Very little has, other than the essential landmarks, highways, and hotels that permit me to navigate from the airport to the Arizona State Prison Complex. The drive from Phoenix into the desert to visit my brother inevitably leaves me barren. As the geography ossifies, I undergo a spiritual desiccation that leaves me feeling as blighted as the sand-swept landscape.

Phoenix is a city of mud. Not just the proliferation of squat, traditional, brick and earth buildings. Even the modern structures seem unable to disguise their adobe ancestry. Some openly embrace it—office buildings whose earthen tones and neo-Native patterned trim are slick nods at the city's indigenous cultures. Others—the hypermodern, black-glass skyscrapers and polished chrome corporate complexes—seem almost willfully anomalous. Outrageous antipodes whose deliberate rejection of anything remotely terraneous serves, through stark opposition, as a further reminder of the city's mud legacy. A divine potter's toy village. Some Great Spirit squatting in his vast sandbox, making mudpies and firing them in geodesic molds; huge cookie cutter blocks and towers laid out in a haphazard desert playground, randomly interrupted by shiny, corny metal trinkets from the great hardware store in the sky.

Easy to imagine, as you drive away from town and the cityscape dissolves into dust, that one careless swipe of a cosmic hand could collapse the whole town, reduce it to a giant palm print the way a sand castle trampled at the beach retains only the shape of your frantic feet. Easy to take the game one step further, begin to believe the countless cacti, the parodic stick-men of the desert, have congregated expressly to bear mute witness to just such an event. Silent sentries determined to keep their vigil till the destruction is complete.

This picture easy to paint because the journey to the jail wreaks this precise havoc on me. Complete emotional compression. My spirit feels stepped on. Stripped and flayed, reduced to rubble. The drive is less than two hours, but seems interminable. It always feels like I'm about to career off the edge of the earth when at last the electric fences come into view and I know I'm almost there. I'm reminded of words one translator used to describe the utter isolation, the obscene remoteness of the rock Zeus chose for Prometheus' exile: "a desolate, lunar landscape; a barren craggy corner of the Caucasus." Worse than the middle of nowhere. The place nowhere forgot.

Maybe that's why I never registered the Gila Reservation. Never occurred to me there might be anybody or anything else out there. Hard to imagine even a jail existing in such a remote place, let alone a "free" community. But there it was, complete with signs advertising "the best fry bread in Arizona." It was my wife who pointed it out, insisted we stop on the way back to Phoenix after a day at the prison. She is from Sierra Leone, West Africa, and despite nearly five years in this country still retains an outsider's perspective, evidenced in this case by a foreigner's bewilderment at the utter erasure of the original people of this continent, her curiosity buttressed by a deep sense of identification with the Native American celebration of and reverence for the land.

Wearily, I agreed to the detour, and we soon found ourselves inside a nearly empty "museum," which was just a gift shop with a few exhibits lined up across the back of the room. One was a replication of a Gila home; a simple canvas-topped lean-to designed to do little but keep out heat and grit. On the far wall, tucked away in the corner of the room, was a large, framed black-and-white still shot of what looked like a military barracks. I moved closer to read the caption, which turned out to be a two-page historical essay pinned bare to the wall.

The "barracks" in the picture was a military camp after all, but unlike any I might have imagined. It turns out the U.S. government had conveniently "re-appropriated" a large portion of the reservation for use as an internment camp for Japanese Americans during World War II (shouldn't that pernicious epithet "Indian-giver" be stricken from the dictionary and replaced with the more historically efficacious "Congress-giver"?). The camp was set along-side the Gila River, from whence the tribe derived not just its name but its life source. Water *is* the Creator in the desert, and the river was the divine axis of the Gila cosmos. Community life took shape through a profound and constant relationship of symbiosis with water, beginning with the sophisticated and elaborate network of irrigation canals the Gila cultivated that nourished an ecosystem that supplied all their needs.

From the account given in the fraying essay, life for the Japanese Americans locked up in that camp was horrific. Lack of resources combined with the war-whipped xenophobia of the American soldiers made it a pretty miserable place. Eventually, military indifference degenerated into outright negligence, and it seems the only way the prisoners survived was through the grace and generosity of the Gila, who supplied them with basic foodstuffs as well as a crash course in desert horticulture so that eventually gardens sprouted in the camp and people were able to eke out a marginal existence.

Relations between the Japanese Americans and the Gila stayed remarkably cordial despite a devastating irony. The prisoners, like those in camps throughout the West and Southwest, were forced into hard labor to support the war effort. At the Gila River camp, this eventually consisted of forcibly usurping, expanding, and rerouting the existing irrigation arrangements; funneling the water away from tribal land to supply the nearest town, a parched and dying bird desperately trying to find its wings and incarnate the potential hibernating in its hopeful moniker: Phoenix.

The project was a spectacular success, of course. Phoenix is flourishing and the Gila River is no more. Outside the museum a dry ditch curves aimlessly through the parking lot, across the highway, and off into the netherland of tumbleweeds that stretches as far as the eye can see. The river has been reduced to a speed bump at the end of a road nobody really uses anymore. The reservation a ghost town, the only inhabitants seem to be those baking fry bread and those watching the gift shop cash register.

Driving back to the city I began to pay attention to signs and convergences that I'd missed during ten years of peregrinations in the desert. The landscape is not all monolithic wasteland. If you're looking for it, you can't miss it. There is literally a line drawn in the sand—as you pass the sign "Leaving Gila Reservation" the first powerlines appear, along with the first evidence of water—a field of what appears to be a species of cotton, which abets a retirement-resort community dotted with grassy lawns. Civilization. The more I looked the more startling the juxtapositions became, poverty and plenty, everything exacerbated by the neutral, flat expanse of the terrain; the palette on which the portrait began to take shape. Somehow this was different, more urgently unsettling than similar abrupt transformations I'd witnessed in urban landscapes. Driving through the mansions of Hyde Park in Chicago and turning onto 47th Street, like finding Beirut down a Beverly Hills alley. But for some strange reason, reconciling carnage and rationalizing hypocrisy was much easier for me in the concrete canyons of a city than hard by the Grand Canyon herself. Both scenes tragically eloquent testaments to America's chilling habit of reverting to diffidence in the face of devastation. Two contemporary episodes in our country's long-standing tradition of schadenfreude—always the unofficial national bloodsport, but never before the era of *Jerry Springer, Rescue 911, Cops,* so clearly our national pastime as well.

———

The first time I ever heard of the internment camps was from my tenth grade history teacher, who was a Japanese American. It wasn't in the classroom—our textbooks didn't mention them—but on the basketball court. Mr. S— was the coach of the sophomore team and as a 4′10″ man had a unique appreciation for small point guards, which endeared me to him. In turn, I was always mesmerized by his gift for masterful storytelling. His voice was rough—crunched gravel—but his tone when telling tales a wonderfully hypnotic blend, invoking soldierly authority and self-deprecation simultaneously. He could be ruthlessly graphic and quietly restrained in the same sentence.

I remember vividly the day at basketball practice when he pulled me aside and for no apparent reason began to tell me about being locked up with his family in a camp in California. I remember being frightened at the depth of bitterness he revealed, and at how this story was so different than any I'd heard him tell, spilling out of him in awkward spurts. I also recall my confusion about the word he kept using to describe the camp. Somehow I heard "interment" instead of "internment," neither of which were words I knew. When I got home and looked up "interment" and saw it referred to burial I was perplexed. The only war camps I'd heard of where people got buried were the concentration camps and Mr. S— was far from Jewish. Even after he explained the distinction to me, I always conjured an image of mass graves and burials at any mention of the Japanese American prisons.

I hadn't thought of that story for years, but it surfaced abruptly the day we visited the Gila museum. I began thinking about burials and forgotten territory and their role in the narratives of justice we tell ourselves and teach our children. How what we leave out is so much more crippling than what we leave in. The dimensions of absence and the territory of silence are the critical spaces in our collective American story.

A prison plopped down in barren, forgotten ground. My brother, the story he's lived and all the stories he might tell buried there, along with too many others'. The legacy of atrocity, American-style; the whole sordid tale of the internment camps buried in desolate corners of dark rooms like the Gila museum. The "reservation" really an "internment camp" for Native Americans; sanitized by language, rebaptized by those possessing the power of nommo. The museum itself, then, interred behind prison walls. And the Gila River: buried in the sand, its history comfortably concealed in the underground pipes that spirit its detritus away to fatten Phoenix.

This is the new tradition. It is no longer fashionable to imprison in full view, we now banish to the far-flung corners of the earth. We can observe a historical migration of prisons from urban centers (the age of the jailhouse right downtown by the courthouse and the fire station; the jail as "hub" of the city) to rural margins and desert hinterlands.

The way a society distances itself from physical structures whose purpose is to hide uncomfortable truths or bury undesirable "necessities" mirrors the way narratives of history and justice bury, evade, and marginalize. The techniques a culture employs for forgetting are the same whether the territory to be forgotten is architectural or anecdotal. Look at which communities house our nuclear and toxic waste dumps. Look at where we put our reservations, internment camps and prisons. Look at how beautifully colonial Williamsburg has been restored and how conveniently marginal or absent are the slave quarters, the amputating axes, the whips and nooses and hanging trees. How easy is it to visit majestic Mt. Vernon; how difficult to find the auction blocks?

Difficult to keep the anger from seeping in, the same bitterness Mr. S — must have tasted on his tongue when he tried to tell me his story. The acid burn that frightened and unnerved me so much those many years ago now threatening to overwhelm the simple story I'm trying to tell today. Perhaps the legacy of our many burials is that we must now endure the putrescence of exhumation.

A skin not considered equal, a meteor has more right than my people
who be wasting time screaming who they've hated
that's why the native tongues has officially been reinstated.
DE LA SOUL, "STAKES IS HIGH"

I recently finished editing an anthology of writings by young black men. There are more than thirty contributors, representing a diverse range of socioeconomic backgrounds and hailing from all over the country—filmmakers, lawyers, journalists, psychologists, students, ex-gangbangers, musicians; fathers, sons, married, single, gay, straight—we run the gamut. So many different voices and visions, harmonizing with and arguing against each other; celebrating the remarkable fullness of our humanity, our plurality and uniqueness; everybody with their own special story to tell.

But we all had one story in common. Each and everyone of us has been detained by the police for DWB: driving while black. This is one of the stories embedded in the folk homonym; the literal and grim reality that in America today too often narratives of justice reveal statistics of just *us*. Fortunately, my conversations with the brothers who submitted to *Soulfires* about getting stopped had a light-hearted tone—they were, after all, survivors' tales. Still, I couldn't help marveling at how mundane this violation has become. The experience of being harassed, mistakenly identified as "criminal," beaten, or wrongfully arrested by police is so commonplace, so universally a part of coming of age for young black men in this country that we can even begin to classify a "trope" of "police narratives" in black male discourse; the way slave narratives have been pegged as the dominant trope of eighteenth- and nineteenth-century black autobiography.

One series of DWB's stands out on my record, maybe because I wasn't driving during any of the incidents. During my sophomore year at Brown, a series of rapes occurred on and around the campus in Providence. Using testimony compiled from several of the survivors' descriptions, police released this description of the suspect: "a 5'8"–5'10" light-skinned black or Hispanic male, possibly wearing a moustache." At the time, this description fit me to a T. My friends would probably have offered it nearly verbatim if I vanished and they had to file a missing persons report. I was stopped by police while walking around town seventeen times over the next two weeks, despite the fact that I immediately, though with much chagrin, scraped the fuzz from my upper lip. But the real story was that Tyrone, the 6'8", purple-black, backup center on the basketball team was stopped almost as often. As was John, who though he'll deny it and try to whup my ass if he reads this, ain't but 5'2". And coffee-bean colored to boot. The Providence police had themselves their own paper-bag party, and declared open season on everyone who couldn't pass the traditional litmus test.

Remarkably, however, there was a get-out-of-jail-free card. A valid Brown University I.D. Flash your campus card and they would let you go, no questions asked. The popular predilection to see black skin as synonymous with guilt and to assume monstrosity, criminality, and deceit, could be obviated by simply wearing your college credentials pinned to your lapel. Though I'm sure this was a position of compromise reached between university administrators and the city cops, it is difficult to ignore the historical continuities, to chalk them up to sheer coincidence.

Black bodies have always been subject to white whim; the "reading" of black lives historically unburdened by any obligations of independent and impartial consideration. Black autobiography has traditionally been dependent on a white authenticating presence, from Phyllis Wheatly's oral interrogation by European skeptics; to the sanctioning of slave narratives by including the testimony, usually in the form of an oath-introduction, of white benefactors or mentors; to the power contemporary publishing houses wield over which black lives get thrust in the face of mainstream America.

My two-week odyssey at Brown evoked stark reminders of one other tradition of white authentication—the phenomenon of "free papers." Free papers were the documents obtained from either former masters or local magistrates that served as legal testament to one's "free" status. Blacks in both the South and the North carried free papers, which theoretically (though they were routinely ignored) protected them from bounty hunters and others who would sell them back into slavery. For a couple weeks that semester, brothers on campus adopted a new benediction, admonishing when we passed each other, "Got'cha papers on you, man?" A running joke, but also an infuriating reminder that our narratives, our words and claims—even in the 1990s—are worthless without the legitimizing presence of white institutional sanction.

If justice in America is one long narrative we are still in the process of constructing, then we must recognize that within the confines of that story one motif, perhaps the most debilitating one for African Americans, is that our role in this country was scripted. Our potential and destiny was already written into the master narrative when we arrived—chattel slaves, pack mules, three-fifths a human being—whereas the fundamental attraction of America for the rest of the world was that it allowed an opportunity to live an unscripted life. A life free of scripture and stricture. Emigration to America imbued rights of authorship—each man free to write his own script, invent his own life. Part of the power of authorship is the power to write your own rules and enforce them, to harness the power of the word to military might. Thus the primal acts that inscribed you as a citizen of the new world (an autonomous author) were voting and bearing arms. The right to write and, if pen did not prove mightier than sword, the means and privilege to tote both and draw either indiscriminately. We enjoyed no such powers. We could not officially script our lives, so we developed the most sophisticated sense of subversive narration in the world: We acquired an enduring fascination and proficiency with the insurrectionary properties of language.

Our narratives of justice are steeped in this tradition, which echoes in jokes about free papers, in proclamations of "just us," in the stories and visions the thirty young men I met shared with each other and the world. Even in, or perhaps *especially* in, the interstices of forgotten territory, the tattered sheafs of buried testimonies, the imprisoned and excavated memories, blowing across and flowing beneath distant desert sands.

JUSTICE: A PERSPECTIVE

I am an old man in a white month. Snow has been falling for years. I borrow a neighbor's extension ladder and lean it against the side of my house. It's way past time for cleaning snow off my roof. Yesterday's newspaper printed a warning issued by the Department of Safety informing citizens that more snow's expected, wet, heavy snow, and roofs may begin collapsing under its weight.

So I prop Mickey's ladder over the side garage door and, shovel in hand, climb. Gingerly, terrified, excited. Wet soles of old sneakers slippery as banana peels on the aluminum rungs. Climb till the steeply pitched roof with its three-foot crest of snow fills my field of vision. Tons of snow up here, a sleeping avalanche the first blow of the shovel will awaken.

Blue sky, glaring whiteness, a few wisps of snow in the air, leftovers from the last storm or scouts of storm coming. Stillness and calm when I'm as high as I dare, flattened against the portion of the ladder that juts into thin air, toes on the last rung below the bib of gutter upon which the ladder rests.

Will I fall? Will my heart burst from overexertion? This scraping and heaving the last thing I'll do with my life? What's going to happen really doesn't worry me. This silliness of clearing snow from a roof when more snow is imminent as good as any way to die. Nothing morbid about my mood, the moment. In fact I feel exhilarated. Yes. Above it all. Reduced in scale and pretension by great white walls towering above me, I could be Cortez gazing for the first time at the Pacific. In a desert two thousand miles away, yellow blooms I mistake for birds pinioned to the spiky tips of a cactus. Armies of cacti, limbs upflung in postures of despair and surrender line the ridges, the washes, gullies, hills, and buttes of a harsh landscape whose undulations are the music I make tossing and turning in my bed.

Yesterday, foolishly, in the semidark of late afternoon, when a sliver of moon hung dimly in the sky, I attacked this same spot, above the garage door where the sloping roofs of master bedroom and rec room intersect. Atop my own rickety wooden stepladder, balanced on the warning label, "Danger: Do not stand above this step," I hacked at the gutters with hatchet and crowbar. Icy shrapnel peppered my face. Tears stung my eyes when I rammed the fist gripping the hatchet into a wind-sculpted bumper of ice.

Picture me chopping and prying, wearing sunglasses that protected my eyes but also just about blinded me. Picture me in the gathering gloom, in a pricey suburban subdivision on a stepladder set beside my nice, big house, determined to free the roof of ice and snow so the roof won't cave in, so the thaw when it arrives won't force melting snow backwards, perversely up and under the shingles, seeping through roofboards, soaking insulation, pooling between rafters, penetrating sheetrock, finally drip, drip, dripping through textured ceilings of master bedroom, upstairs bath, and downstairs front hall as it did last time this much snow, corralled by ice, collected on my roof. Picture me picturing myself, once a poor black boy, finally, in spite of the odds, grown-up, risking life and limb again to do the right thing. Picture me imagining myself on the ground, slowly regaining consciousness, attempting to explain to a passerby why I'm buried half-dead in a snowdrift.

Yesterday, on that day we're picturing—stepladder too short, darkness to thick, afraid of falling, mad at nature, mad at whatever it was inside myself rousting me outdoors in freezing weather to perform a task against my will and better judgment—the worse thing about that day was the certainty, even as I spread the stepladder's legs and humped up and down to anchor its invisible feet in thigh deep snow, the worst thing I felt was the certainty of failure.

Now, today, on this new morning, in the sunlight, on my neighbor's ladder the job feels infinitely doable—my efforts will be rewarded, justice served.

I luxuriate in the view from twenty feet up. Welcome the immensity of a brilliant blue sky that puts the ominous glare of my little snow-drowned roof in perspective. Through my neighbor's window I can see the dollhouse tranquility, the good intentions of their tastefully furnished rooms. This whole business of risking my life to clear a roof is okay because I've adjusted my perspective. Worked out a new slant on things.

Everything depends on perspective. And luckily there's a science of perspective to depend upon. A science highly developed by painters of the fifteenth century. Treatises exist on the subject. How-to manuals for aspiring artists. One essential prop in the development of this science of perspective was the camera obscura, a dark room or box in which light entered only through a pinprick in one end, causing the view through the peephole to appear as an image on the black wall opposite. Just as we apply laws to simulate justice, scientists and artists evolved rules for organizing a picture of the world as it appeared when burnt as an image on a flat surface. Not the world these scientists and artists experienced every day, but the world reduced, imprisoned, reflected inside the camera obscura. The laws of linear perspective the theorists delineated were laws for reproducing a copy of a copy. Forgotten, ignored, or undiscussed was the willed blindness within the black box, the hood over the head, the problematic relationship of camera obscura images to what a human eye and heart know even if the eye's peering from inside a box at the sea of light beyond its cage.

Infatuated by the way the scenes reproduced inside the camera obscura could be replicated by mechanical, mathematically precise coordinates, most painters junked other experiments for expressing the mystery of perception and apprenticed themselves to the technology of linear perspective, the trick of rendering three dimensions on a flat surface. They forsook the floating indeterminacy of medieval manuscript illuminations and tapestries, put on hold the continuous give-and-take between an object and its image in the mind. Painting inferred the stability and consequence of a material world, a world the spirit knew as illusion and chaos, the field of play for memory, dream, desire.

The result: a world imagined through a window, *out there,* separate from the viewer, a justly proportioned, settled thing for the artist to mirror. An unspoken pact was forged between painting and audience: The version of reality revealed by the keyhole of the camera obscura became Real. The gorgeous spectacle of Renaissance art ensued. But no gain without pain. The picture frame excludes as it includes. Television the latest blip on the wall masquerading as an equivalence for the light in us, around us, containing us, contained by us, where time, space, motion, the gods dance.

I mention all that only to say no science of perspective accounts for the desert, for the dagger I see before me, hanging in the air, the dagger's handle, the desert's punctured yellow blooms bidding me close my fingers around them.

Here is what I mean. My wife, who in middle middle age is teaching herself computers, said a couple days ago it's almost refreshing how regularly, brutally computers remind you that you learn only by committing mistakes. You type away, doing what you usually do, type, typing, and then the machine goes haywire, nothing is happening the way it should and you have no idea why, but you know you must stop and adjust, figure out the mistake you've committed and rectify it if you want to resume type, typing.

Nine years ago, a week ago, a second ago my son lost control of the howling chaos inside him he'd been struggling with fiercely, silently, alone, for most of his sixteen years to quell. He was touring the western states in a chaperoned group of sixteen-year-olds, boys who'd attended summer camp together over the years. After a long, frustrating day in a rental car, a day of minor mishaps and wrong turns, the party had stopped overnight in an Arizona motel near the Grand Canyon.

There are many versions of what happened that night. Given the consequences of whatever happened, no version is very pretty. From my perspective, the one from this desk, from the snow-smothered rooftop I'm recalling, it's enough to say the boy sleeping in a cabin with my son was killed and my son fled. After a week of running, my son phoned home, and my wife and I flew to Phoenix to accompany him when he turned himself in to the police.

To decide what occurred that terrible night in an Arizona motel, the state was obliged to construct a picture, freeze-frame, and simplify events to render them in terms of the law. Like a scene achieved by an artist copying an image focused through the camera obscura, the picture the state painted was arbitrary, omitting far more than it included, disclosing a lot about the law's blind spots, its arbitrariness, how law dismembers, tears apart living tissue. In the name of justice, the state put its fearsome weight behind the view of things stipulated by the coordinates of law. From the state of Arizona's perspective, my son deserved to be treated as a hardened criminal rather than a good kid who for unaccountable reasons had snapped one night and needed help not punishment; he was tried as an adult rather than a juvenile and sentenced to life imprisonment.

The above summary mercifully leaves out a multitude of pertinent, mind-boggling, soul-crushing details. Some of these details would come to you as no surprise. Others you'd never guess, even if you tried harder than would be wise to imagine the devastation visited upon families by the loss of one young, promising life, the blighting of another.

At sixteen my son found himself suddenly transformed from a privileged, middle-class teenager growing up in a small town, attending high school, to a caged beast, hunted, baited, condemned. This required of him, of course, a change in perspective.

Required the same of his mother, brother and sister, me. I cannot speak for other members of my family, but in the nine years since my son's been in prison, I've managed no satisfactory adjustment of perspective. No notion of justice I've been able to formulate makes sense of a boy's death in Arizona, my son's sentencing and incarceration.

There is a space I need to fill when I try to write *justice,* but the space remains. I recall what my wife said about computers and making mistakes. Only this isn't like confronting a mistake and pushing buttons until the computer stops printing out a stigmata of dots, dashes, and symbols. This emptiness is more like constant bleeding. Like typing along with continuously disturbing results, sometimes far worse than others, but never really getting it close to right. Incriminating errors, painful errors, but continuing on and on, not because time heals or familiarity dulls the ache or because I think I'm getting away with anything or believe that my story unraveling in fits and starts, with dangerous, yawning gaps, is all right. I go on because I skip the space where justice should fit. Yearn for it to be filled, but keep climbing. Like some terminally ill patients long for the peace and rest they believe follows death. Yearn for the fall. Keep climbing.

Up on the housetop, click click click / Down the chimney comes Old Saint Nick. I was one of those kids who believed in Santa Claus way past the time everybody else in the crowd had put old Santa to sleep. I was his defender. Got a tooth loosened in a fistfight once protecting his honor. Impossible not to remember him up here where I am, staring at the apex of my roof, the snow-draped stone chimney astraddle it. I loved you, you bloody, jellyroll elf. Your fluffy white beard, blue sky eyes, your plump, alkie's cheeks, your scarlet longjohns with snowy muffs of fur decorating the cuffs. Remember the time in Kaufmann's department store I climbed on your knee and the snapshot my mom paid two of my daddy's hard-earned quarters for was nothing but a blaze of light where our heads should have been. Ha, ha. Vampire, motherfucker. No reflection in the mirror. Biting off my head so I disappear too.

Here is what I mean. In the Arizona desert where they keep him you can see forever. Flat, flat to the pale, scalloped crust of mountains that might be as far away as the farthest edge of the earth, far as the moon. So distant your eye travels once around the world and back to the very spot where you're standing wondering how far away those mountains might be. You are a point, infinitesimal on that vast loop of trying to see what's out there, trying to ascertain where you stand in relationship to the emptiness surrounding you. Think of many lines emanating from the point where you are fixed, lines like laws, like the threads artists stretched across their canvases to locate the vanishing point, visible coordinates of perspective matching the lines drawn on the image produced inside the camera obscura. Lines multiplying till they form a solid sphere, like a skein of yarn wound round and round itself. You are a smaller speck on the giant ball than the invisible point where all lines converge, melt. The busyness of your gaze seeking, casting about, tracking, scanning, trying to make sense, imaging questions and answers, alternate scenarios, the restless, hungry gasps of your eyes print the numberless lines that locate you, cage you, here, nowhere, nothing in the desert where they keep him.

Reality in this desert is what's meant to elude you. The sum of your mistakes, minus them. Why you never see things clearly. Why I fail to adjust and gain perspective. In this desert the sand is grains of justice delayed, justice denied, the long, slow, proverbial arc of justice pulverized when it touches down to earth.

When it snows in the desert those low slung silhouettes on the horizon, mottled bluish and dusk, compounds of shadow and sandstone and granite and cloud, inch closer. Hunker down, staring vigilant-eyed, as near as they dare to the campfire. They lie there just beyond what they know is the circle of your effectiveness, where even if you charged at them, no way you'd catch them. How close they seem, how tame and absent, the twin mirrors of their eyes unblinking. When it snows, the long view shrinks to this intimate sharing, sharing the last dregs of heat, scraps of food, the moon. If you howl, that too will be shared, return to you as echo, burn like red cinders in your throat.

One day in the desert snow falls, a marvel, a chance to live a different life with new rules and conclusions. Sand puckers like a textured ceiling, leaks sprout, a forest of straight, transparent stems shoot up, magnified by close-up, time-lapse trick photography that collapses seasons into seconds. The bars of rain crystallize, shatter, become white flakes falling. The floor of the desert turns over in its sleep, rises, spreads its thorny arms to receive pale blossoms.

I think of this New England spring storm as a fist. I must pry open its stiff, frozen fingers and see what it's done to my house. So I take a deep breath and get on with it, start to chip and chop, pray I don't go dancing off into the frigid air, falling up, picturing myself ridiculous and dead before I hit the ground.

The ladder tips. Oh, shit. It's the Big One, ladies and gentlemen. My neighbor's two-hundred-foot aluminum extension firetruck rescue 911 naked people from blazing skyscrapers at night in a snowstorm ladder slides sideways down the blister of ice it's resting on, a slide I precipitate by cracking with my shovel the pouting lip of ice anchoring the blister. Sliding. Slow enough for me to know what's going to happen, fast enough so I'm helpless to change it.

Amazing how rapidly the mind shuttles through alternate perspectives in this kind of crisis situation. You know what I mean. Welcoming, disregarding, inventing, recalling. Line after smoke-tailed line of possibilities propelled into space. Futile as all the harpoons chasing Moby Dick, but incredibly quick. A thousand lives you might have lived and all the ones you've lived already, all the combinations and permutations of what might come and what's gone flash through your mind as the ladder shifts, a tiny wobble just below the threshold of your awareness, then something you are remembering because it must have happened—that tilt, shift, that lean, that sly, told-you-so smile—to commence the ride you're on.

Too much weight to bear. Your big, sweat-suited body way up here, pinned to the ladder's tip. For a millisecond you understand why snow and sand are the same thing. Fire and ice indistinguishable in a blow you dealt your thumb. Justice sleeps. You will not be saved. Nothing happens next. You crash through your neighbor's roof, a visitor from another planet screaming apologies in a language no one understands because nobody's home.

CONTRIBUTORS

JULIA ALVAREZ is a poet and fiction writer. Her poetry collections include *Homecoming* and *The Housekeeping Book*, and, most recently, *The Other Side/El Otro Lado*. Her novels are *How the Garcia Girls Lost Their Accents* and *In the Time of the Butterflies*, which was a finalist for the National Book Critics Award in 1995. She teaches creative writing and literature at Middlebury College.

RICHARD BAUSCH is the author of seven novels and four short story collections, including the novels *Rebel Powers* and *Violence* and the story collections *The Fireman's Wife, Rare and Endangered Species*, and *Selected Stories*. His novel *Good Evening Mr. and Mrs. America, and All the Ships at Sea* was published in Fall 1996. He is Heritage Professor of Writing at George Mason University.

MADISON SMARTT BELL is the author of eight novels, including *The Washington Square Ensemble, Waiting for the End of the World, The Year of Silence, Doctor Sleep*, and *Soldier's Joy*, as well as two collections of short stories, *Zero db* and *Barking Man*. His novel *All Soul's Rising* was a finalist for the 1995 PEN/Faulkner and National Book Awards. He is writer-in-residence at Goucher College.

BLANCHE McCRARY BOYD is the author of a book of essays, *The Redneck Way of Knowledge,* and three novels, *Mourning the Death of Magic, The Revolution of Little Girls* and *Terminal Velocity.* Her journalism has appeared in a number of publications, most frequently in the *Village Voice.* She is writer-in-residence at Connecticut College.

JOHN CASEY has published a collection of stories, *Testimony and Demeanor.* His novels include *An American Romance* and *Spartina; Spartina* won the National Book Award in 1989 and was a Book Critics Circle nomination in 1990. *Supper at the Black Pearl* is his most recent work. He lives in Charlottesville, Virginia.

MICHAEL DORRIS authored a number of books of fiction and nonfiction, including *Paper Trail* (essays), *The Broken Cord, Working Men Stories, Rooms in the House of Stone,* and *A Yellow Raft in Blue Water.* His most recent works include *Sees Behind the Trees,* a novel for young adults, and *Cloud Chamber.* He died in 1997.

GARRETT HONGO is a poet and essayist and the author of a recent memoir, *Volcano,* about his home village in Hawaii. His books are *Yellow Light* and *The River of Heaven,* which was a finalist for the 1989 Pulitzer Prize in poetry. When not in Hawaii, he is associate professor of English and director of creative writing at the University of Oregon.

CHARLES JOHNSON is the author of three novels, among them *Middle Passage,* which won the National Book Award in 1990, a story collection, *the Sorcerer's Apprentice,* a work of philosophical aesthetics, *Being and Race: Black Writing since 1970,* and two collections of comic art. He is the Pollock Professor of English at the University of Washington.

ALEX KOTLOWITZ is the author of *There Are No Children Here: The Story of Two Boys Growing Up in the Other America.* For ten years he was a staff writer at the *Wall Street Journal,* writing on urban affairs and social policy. He has also contributed to National Public Radio, the *MacNeil/Lehrer NewsHour,* and numerous magazines. His honors include the George Polk Award and the Robert F. Kennedy Journalism Award.

BEVERLY LOWRY is the author of numerous novels, among which are *Emma Blue, Daddy's Girl, Breaking Gentle,* and *The Track of Real Desires,* and the nonfiction book *Crossed Over: A Murder, A Memoir.* Her short stories and journalism have appeared in such publications as the *Black Warrior Review,* the *New York Times,* and *Vanity Fair.* She has taught at the University of Houston and the University of Montana and lives in Washington, D.C.

MARTHA MINOW is a Professor of Law at Harvard Law School, where she teaches family law and civil procedure. She is the author of *Making all the Difference: Inclusion, Exclusion, and American Law,* editor of *Family Matters: Readings on Family Lives and the Law,* and, most recently, coeditor of *Law Stories.*

CLARENCE PAGE, the 1989 Pulitzer Prize winner for Commentary, is a nationally syndicated columnist for the *Chicago Tribune,* as well as a contributor of essays to the *MacNeil/Lehrer NewsHour,* a panelist on Black Entertainment Television's *Lead Story,* and a commentator on National Public Radio's *Weekend Sunday.* He is the author of *Showing My Color: Impolite Essays on Race and Identity.*

SARAH PETTIT is the Editor in Chief of *Out,* the nation's best-selling lesbian and gay men magazine, which she helped found in 1992. She was previously the Arts editor of *OutWeek,* a New York gay and lesbian weekly, and an Assistant Editor for St. Martin's Press. Pettit also helped edit a special issue of *The Nation,* titled "A Queer Nation," and has contributed to *Newsweek.*

NTOZAKE SHANGE, playwright, poet, and novelist, is the author of, among other works, *for colored girls who have considered suicide / when the rainbow is enuf* and *Boogie Woogie Landscapes* (plays); *Ridin' the Moon in Texas* and *The Lore Space Demands* (poetry); *Sassafras, Cypress and Indigo, Betsey Brown,* and *Liliane: Resurrection of the Daughter* (novels). She lives in Philadelphia.

PORTER SHREVE worked at the *Washington Post* for four years before taking a June Rose Colby Fellowship in the University of Michigan's

M.F.A. in creative writing. He lives in Ann Arbor, where he is completing a novel, *The Obituary Writer.*

SUSAN RICHARDS SHREVE is the author of ten novels, among them *Miracle Play, A Country of Strangers, Daughters of the New World,* and, most recently, *The Visiting Physician.* She is an award-winning children's author, with twenty-two books, former President of the PEN/Faulkner Award for Fiction, and coeditor of an essay collection, *Skin Deep: Black Women and White Women Write about Race.* She is a professor of English at George Mason University.

GERALD M. STERN began his career as a trial attorney in the Civil Rights Division of the U.S. Department of Justice trying voter discrimination cases in the South. Later, as lead counsel for over six hundred survivors of a coal mine disaster in West Virginia, he won a multimillion dollar settlement for the victims and wrote a book on the case, *The Buffalo Creek Disaster.* Most recently he was Special Counsel for Financial Institution Fraud and Health Care Fraud at the U.S. Department of Justice.

DANIEL J. WIDEMAN is a writer of fiction and nonfiction. He has published a recent book of nonfiction, *The Door of No Return: A Journey through the Legacy of the African Slave Forts*, and coedited an anthology, *Soulfires: Young Black Men on Love and Violence.* He lives in Durham, North Carolina, where he is completing a novel, *A Ticket 'Til Morning.*

JOHN EDGAR WIDEMAN is a two-time winner of the PEN/Faulkner Award and has been a nominee for the National Book Critics Circle Award and the National Book Award. Among his novels are *Sent for You Yesterday, Philadelphia Fire,* and *The Cattle Killing.* Along with several short story collections, he has written two memoirs, *Brothers and Keepers* and *Fatheralong.* He teaches at the University of Massachusetts in Amherst.